d
ls,
el.

ur
ets
ld,
nce
vel.

**Rely on Thomas Cook as your
travelling companion on your next trip
and benefit from our unique heritage.**

Thomas Cook **pocket** guides

BRUSSELS

Your travelling companion since 1873

Written by Ryan Levitt, updated by Anwer Bati

Published by Thomas Cook Publishing
A division of Thomas Cook Tour Operations Limited
Company registration no. 3772199 England
The Thomas Cook Business Park, Unit 9, Coningsby Road,
Peterborough PE3 8SB, United Kingdom
Email: books@thomascook.com, Tel: +44 (0) 1733 416477
www.thomascookpublishing.com

Produced by Cambridge Publishing Management Limited
Burr Elm Court, Main Street, Caldecote CB23 7NU
www.cambridgepm.co.uk

ISBN: 978-1-84848-350-7

© 2007, 2009 Thomas Cook Publishing
This third edition © 2011 Thomas Cook Publishing
Text © Thomas Cook Publishing
Maps © Thomas Cook Publishing/PCGraphics (UK) Limited
Transport map © Communicarta Limited

Series Editor: Karen Beaulah
Production/DTP: Steven Collins

Printed and bound in Spain by GraphyCems

Cover photography © Pictures Colour Library

Although every care has been taken in compiling this publication, and the contents
are believed to be correct at the time of printing, Thomas Cook Tour Operations
Limited cannot accept any responsibility for errors or omissions, however caused,
or for changes in details given in the guidebook, or for the consequences of any
reliance on the information provided. Descriptions and assessments are based on
the author's views and experiences when writing and do not necessarily represent
those of Thomas Cook Tour Operations Limited.

CONTENTS

SYMBOLS KEY

The following symbols are used throughout this book:

ⓐ address ⓣ telephone ⓦ website address ⓛ opening times
ⓝ public transport connections ⓘ important

The following symbols are used on the maps:

𝒊	information office	◼	point of interest
✈	airport	O	city
✚	hospital	O	large town
Ⓞ	police station	o	small town
🚌	bus station	=	motorway
🚆	railway station	—	main road
Ⓜ	metro	—	minor road
✝	cathedral	—	railway
❶	numbers denote featured cafés & restaurants		

Hotels and restaurants are graded by approximate price as follows:
£ budget price ££ mid-range price £££ expensive

▶ *The EU Parliament building*

 INTRODUCING
Brussels

Introduction

Brussels has always had a bit of a boring reputation. Grey-clad Eurocrats creating annoying legislation, rain-drenched days, bizarre linguistic issues – it's not exactly the picture of a perfect holiday.

Well, it's time to banish your misconceptions and embrace the new Brussels, a city of culinary masterpieces, hot nights of clubbing, art treasures and cutting-edge performance.

Situated less than two hours from London by train, and linked with almost every regional airport in the UK and Ireland, Brussels offers easy connections for those looking for a convenient and intriguing short-break destination. And those with financial limitations can pack their days with a variety of free sights that take in the best of the city.

The Grand Place is the heart of Lower Town. Once described by Victor Hugo (author of *Les Miserables*) as the most beautiful square in Europe, this collection of guild houses in the Italian Baroque style is simply breathtaking. But that's not all there is to see in this historic quarter. There's also the Manneken Pis, a fountain of a peeing boy that is considered a symbol of the city.

Over in Upper Town are royal sights and inspiring galleries, including a fascinating gallery devoted to the history of musical instruments.

And if you thought that the city was all about European culture, you'd be mistaken. A vibrant African population in the ethnically diverse neighbourhood of Ixelles offers great restaurants, markets, bars and clubs for visitors looking for something out of the ordinary. Brussels also has a large Middle-Eastern population.

So forget what you might have heard about Brussels in the past. This city is sprouting with a new vibe and is ready to welcome you with a friendly smile and a glass of its amazing beer. You'll soon be raising a glass to one of Europe's most intriguing cities.

◯ *There's something to see in the Grand Place all year round*

When to go

Brussels is worth visiting at any time of year, since there is always plenty to do and see. For many, the best time to visit is during the summer period when the city really comes alive. At this time of the year live music concerts take over city squares, open-air film screenings draw the masses and the population explodes with excitement.

If what goes on in Brussels itself is not enough, then head off to any of the nearby cities. The cobbled streets of Leuven, the military fascination of Waterloo, and the fast fashion of Antwerp are all enticing in their own right and well worth taking time away from the Belgian capital.

SEASONS & CLIMATE

The climate of Brussels is similar to what you might find in London: often overcast, damp for much of the winter, yet sunny and bright for long periods during the summer. Year-round temperatures seldom drop below 0°C (32°F) or rise above 25°C (77°F).

If you don't mind the chill, winter is a pleasant time to visit for avoiding the tourist crowds. Snow is rarely a consideration, and the winter fogs actually add an atmosphere that makes you feel as if you're in a period film.

In the early spring, the meaning of the old saying 'April showers bring May flowers' becomes clear – but in this city's case the showers can often stretch into June. When summer finally does arrive, the thermometer hovers around the mid-20s°C (70s°F) with occasional heatwaves that usually last no longer than a couple of days. Street activity blossoms during this period as the long days and outdoor cafés create a buzzing atmosphere.

The best season in which to visit in terms of crowds and weather is autumn. The buzz of the streets may be gone, but there are still plenty of things to see and do – and the threat of rain is greatly reduced.

◐ *The famous Carpet of Flowers blooms in the Grand Place*

ANNUAL EVENTS

In Brussels and the surrounding region there are many more events than can be mentioned here – the local tourist offices can provide a full list. ❶ Note that exact dates of events may change from year to year – so check first. ⓦ www.bitc.be gives a comprehensive calendar of events.

March
Brussels International Festival of Fantastic Film Two-week film festival dedicated to horror and sci-fi. Prepare yourself for the gore! Always a lot of fun. Side events such as body-painting exhibits and fetish shows go along for the ride. The final event is a Vampire Ball. Tickets sell out well in advance and you'll only get in if you're wearing a killer costume. ⓦ www.bifff.org

May
Jazz Marathon Non-stop jazz takes over almost all the bars, clubs and stages in the city for three days. Shuttle buses run between the major venues. Each year more than 250,000 people come to listen to the music. Book your hotel room well in advance. ⓦ www.brusselsjazzmarathon.be

June
Battle of Waterloo See the epic battle that destroyed Napoleon re-created on the field where the tides turned against him. Major re-enactments are only held every five years. The next event is scheduled for 2015. ⓦ www.waterloo1815.be

Festival of Flanders/Festival of Wallonia Two festivals, two languages, one big celebration of culture. Classical music is the core focus of both festivals with concerts organised throughout the country. ⓦ www.festivaldewallonie.be, www.festival.be

July
National Day National celebration featuring pageantry, military displays and royal family sightings, held every year on 21 July.

December
Le Marché de Noël Brussels' Christmas market packed with stalls selling *Glühwein* (mulled wine), toys and ornaments runs from the Grand Place to Place Sainte-Catherine, ending at an open-air skating rink. ⓦ www.plaisirsdhiver.be

---

PUBLIC HOLIDAYS
New Year's Day 1 Jan
Easter Sunday 24 Apr 2011; 8 Apr 2012; 31 Mar 2013
Easter Monday 25 Apr 2011; 9 Apr 2012; 1 Apr 2013
Labour Day 1 May
Ascension Day 6th Sun after Easter
Pentecostal Whit Monday 7th Mon after Easter
Battle of the Golden Spurs Holiday in Flanders, 11 July
Belgian National Day 21 July
Assumption 15 Aug
All Saints' Day 1 Nov
Armistice Day 11 Nov
Christmas Day 25 Dec

Ommegang

Relive the Golden Age of the city by joining in the fun of Ommegang. This stately procession re-enacts a similar event that honoured the entry of the Emperor Charles V into the city in 1549 with festivities lasting for three days. Locals dress up as nobles, guildsmen, jesters and any other type of 16th-century resident they can think of.

The procession can be made on horseback or on foot and runs for about 2 km (just over 1 mile) from the Upper Town to the Lower Town, ending at the Grand Place. A grandstand is set up allowing views of the jousting tournament, horse parade and stilt fighting. However, tickets must be booked well in advance. Seats usually sell out about two months prior to the day. If you don't want to fight the crowds, go instead to the cafés on Place du Grand Sablon where you can watch the start of the parade. It's not as visually exciting or as much fun, but you'll get to see everything without the jostling or ticket expense.

The procession is held on the first Thursday of July. However, the party atmosphere lasts through the weekend. Ommegang literally means 'walk around' in Dutch, and that's essentially all you do. Walk around the streets in the procession, walk around from bar to bar, walk around to see your friends – it's a very social and welcoming event. If ever you wanted to see Belgians dissolve their traditionally frosty exterior, then now is the time to visit.

Children love Ommegang because of the medieval re-enactments, colourful garb, flying banners and displays of horsemanship. Adults love what happens after dark when the entire city turns into the scene of the nation's biggest knees-up. As you'd expect, hotel rooms need to be booked well in advance. **ⓐ** Grand Place **ⓣ** 02 512 1961 **ⓦ** www.ommegang.be **ⓘ** Tickets must be pre-booked

ⵔ *Ommegang: fun to watch, even more fun to join in!*

History

The city of Brussels was first mentioned in a 7th-century manuscript. It is thought that the name Brussels came from the Flemish word *Broekzele* (or 'marshland'), as the original foundations of the city were on an island in the River Senne.

Historically, the founding date of the city is attributed to the year 580 when Saint Géry is said to have built a chapel somewhere in the region of the Lower Town. By the 9th century, the town had grown into a prosperous mercantile community ruled by the Franks who overtook the region following the fall of the Roman Empire.

City walls protected the citizens of Brussels from invaders such as the Vikings until the 13th century, when population growth put pressure on the town. Craftsmen moved to the city to assist with construction and trade began to boom. Fabrics and textile making were the chief money-making industries, causing neighbouring forces to note and admire the region's wealth.

At the end of the 14th century, the city was invaded by the Count of Flanders, forcing new fortifications to be built around the city. These fortifications follow the path of the petite ceinture. However, none of the original gates exists today.

A key royal marriage brought the city under the rule of Burgundy, and the city was proclaimed capital of Burgundy in the 1430s. The result was a boom in revenue and trade. This period of peace lasted until 1466 when another royal marriage allowed the ruling Spanish Habsburgs to capture control of the city. Locals hated the Habsburgs and the capital was taken away from the ruling Spanish for a period of about 40 years.

Prosperity reigned during this period until the Reformation divided the city, triggering riots between Catholics and Protestants. The battles continued until the Spanish were defeated by the English (Protestants).

More empires fought for control over this strategically important city. First came the French in 1695, which resulted in the destruction of the Grand Place. The guilds soon rebuilt all the houses and the badly damaged town hall. Next came the Austrians in the early 18th century. Austrian rule ensued and eventually bankrupted the city coffers as the War of the Austrian Succession stripped the city of almost all its assets.

Following the French Revolution, the country's working classes began to revolt against the demands of the Austrian throne. Their struggles resulted in a War of Independence that established the independent nation of Belgium in 1830.

The 20th century continued to be eventful. The city blossomed with the rise of Art Nouveau, only for the Germans to occupy their fledgling state during both world wars despite the country's stated neutrality. The second half of the century saw Belgium lose control of its African colonies, a process fraught with instability.

Ironically, Brussels is now synonymous with stability. The city is at the heart of Europe, home to both the European Union and NATO, and a leading force in politics and business. The 2010 elections, however, emphasised the differences between Separatist Flanders and Socialist Wallonia.

Lifestyle

As they live in the heart of northern Europe, and have a strong tradition of trade and travel, Belgians exhibit characteristics commonly associated with neighbouring nations – and combine those traits into something truly unique.

Say the word 'Europe' and residents will be the first to complain about rising housing costs, expenditure on public services, overcrowding and traffic. On the quiet, however, it's a different matter, as Belgians love the idea of being considered the unofficial capital country of the EU. Due to years of invasion, Belgians truly do represent Europe. Where one local will exhibit Nordic features that recall Scandinavian and Dutch influences in the country, another will look almost Spanish – yet both will be Belgian through and through.

TRADITIONS AND ETIQUETTE

Belgians have a reputation for following unspoken northern European codes of practice to mind their own business and keep their front doors firmly shut. This belief may be partly true. Some people say that trying to prise an invitation out of a Belgian to visit their family home is a bit like trying to find Willy Wonka's golden ticket; but get them out of the house and locals are just as generous, exciting and talkative as the next person. Their apparent habit of zealously protecting their privacy is somewhat rooted in history.

The one thing that binds Belgians together, and is a constant source of discussion and debate, is the separation of Dutch-speaking Flanders from French-speaking Wallonia. Like a couple who have been married too long (yet can't live without each other), the two linguistically divided halves of the country are constantly at odds. Yet, when the country was formed in 1830, these two communities elected to stay together rather than run the risk of independence. Deep down, both the Flemish and the Walloons have read their history books and know that they are better off together, despite recent tensions.

◆ *Place Sainte-Catherine is a lovely spot to unwind*

Culture

Belgians are big supporters of the arts, both contemporary and classic. This is not one of those countries whose people will only attend performances of old favourites or historically important plays. Rather, residents eagerly await cutting-edge modern dance and contemporary music with a fervour unmatched anywhere else in Europe.

While the nobility of Belgium haven't always been huge fans, classical music has thrived in Brussels. Major works by such leading lights as Stravinsky and Bartók premiered in this city, and the **La Monnaie/De Munt** theatre (ⓐ Place de la Monnaie ⓣ 02 229 1200 ⓦ www.lamonnaie.be) is back with a vengeance.

Because Belgium has more than one official language, public funding is stretched to its limits. For every Flemish company there must be an equivalent French version. The end result is that organisations with promise fall by the wayside as they struggle to keep up with financial obligations. Despite this fact, concert-goers have reason to rejoice as world-class festivals revive their spirits every May in the form of the **Concours Musical International Reine Elisabeth de Belgique** (Queen Elisabeth International Music Competition of Belgium ⓦ www.cmireb.be). Founded in 1937, this annual festival has a rotating schedule concentrating on violin, piano, composition and vocal performance. The final gala is always sold out, drawing an audience from across the linguistic divide.

While locals are huge consumers of contemporary art, they tend to avoid the galleries of Belgium in favour of the more noted spaces of London, New York and Berlin. This refusal to

⬤ *Children will love the famous Toone puppet theatre*

purchase local work isn't due to a lack of talent. Rather, it's because there are so few commercial galleries in the city. If you are determined to check out what's on offer, plan your visit around the **Brussels Art Fair** held each spring (ⓦ www.artexis.com).

Most theatrical performance in Brussels is in French or Dutch. For the best options, check out the programming at the Théâtre National (see page 70). For experimental work, go instead to the **Beursschouwburg** (ⓦ www.beursschouwburg.be), and mix with the hip and happening audience. English-language theatre troupes abound in Brussels but strictly at an amateur level. Companies to look out for include the American Theater Company, English Theatre Brussels, Brussels Light Opera Company and Brussels Shakespeare Society.

Dance-wise, Brussels leads the world as an innovator and producer of influential modern choreography. Classical work may be the speciality of the renowned **Royal Ballet of Flanders** (ⓦ www.koninklijkballetvanvlaanderen.be), but it's the cutting-edge work of companies such as the **Rosas** company (ⓦ www.rosas.be), under the direction of Anne Teresa de Keersmaeker, and Frédéric Flamand's Charleroi Danse that truly excite and energise.

◗ *The Grand Place buildings in all their splendour*

MAKING THE MOST OF
Brussels

Shopping

In Belgium, each city has its specialities and treats. Antwerp is known for its high fashion, and Ghent for its lace. In Brussels it's all about the food: sinfully sweet chocolate, organic meats and vegetables, creamy cheeses and bottles of delicious beer. For truly exotic products, the ethnic streets of Ixelles offer plenty of opportunities for shopping sensations; otherwise explore the one-off offerings of the shops of the historic Lower Town for the finest in food and drink.

While big shopping centres aren't a standard feature of the city's streets, there are covered arcades known as *galeries*, very similar to the arcades of London. These quiet mini-malls boast unique boutiques of designer fashions and speciality goods that are high on price and quality. The best known is **Les Galeries Royales Saint-Hubert** (❷ Rue du Marché-aux-Herbes), located slightly northeast of the Grand Place.

For true treasures, head down to the Place du Jeu de Balle in the heart of the working-class neighbourhood of Les Marolles where a flea market has been held since 1873. The market beckons shoppers every single day of the week with its collection of jewels and junk. You'll have to hunt long and hard for finds – but when you strike gold, you'll experience a high that's difficult to match.

If you prefer your shopping experiences to be less stressful, go instead to the more salubrious antiques centre at **Passage 125** (❷ Rue Blaes 125). This large warehouse is tucked in between a slew of restored furniture shops and offers the collections of more than 25 top-notch dealers, all of whom can arrange worldwide shipping.

⬤ *Some things are not meant to last*

USEFUL SHOPPING PHRASES

What time do the shops open/close?
A quelle heure ouvrent/ferment les magasins?
Ah kehl ur oovr/fehrm leh mahgazang?

How much is this?
C'est combien?
Cey combyahng?

Can I try this on?
Puis-je essayer ceci?
Pweezh ehssayeh cerssee?

My size is...
Ma taille (clothes)/
ma pointure (shoes) est ...
*Mah tie/mah
pooahngtewr ay ...*

I'll take this one, thank you
Je prends celui-ci/celle-ci merci
*Zher prawng serlweesi/
sehlsee mehrsee*

If you're looking for big names, fear not. With so many Eurocrat shoppers and their spouses in town, you can guarantee that there is a lot of Gucci and Versace to go around. Avenue Louise and the Boulevard du Waterloo are the streets to head for if your idea of shopping comes with a six-figure price tag!

Eating & drinking

Belgium has more Michelin-starred chefs per capita than virtually any other country on the planet. Combine that with the seemingly endless expense accounts of the Eurocrat brigade and what you have is a dining scene that is simply beyond compare. Belgian food is a combination of French cuisine – often covered in sauce – fresh seafood, and hearty German and Dutch fare.

Locals are picky when it comes to ingredients, as the nation's mercantile past has brought the flavours of the world to them, and residents know their culinary stuff. Not for them the tasteless fruit and veg of a typical British supermarket. Flavour is where it's at, meaning that seasonality and freshness are prized above all.

Food has been a valued part of daily life for centuries. Belgians have long had a reputation for being hard-working yet keen to celebrate when the occasion arises. The best reward for them after a long day at the office is a well-prepared meal – and they will work long and hard to ensure that only the best is dished up.

The cuisine of Brussels is heavily influenced by the flavours of its regions. Fresh seafood from the coast, game from the Ardennes, rich sauces from Wallonia and, of course, beer.

PRICE CATEGORIES

Price ratings given in this book are based on the cost of a main course at dinner, including tax and service.
£ up to €15   ££ €15–35   £££ over €35

What really differentiates the cooking of Brussels from that of other regions of Belgium is its variety. Nowhere else in the country has such a large ethnic community offering the flavours of the Congo, Asia, the Middle East and India.

The mussels of Brussels no longer come from Belgian waters. The best varieties come from nearby Dutch ports and many signs will advertise this fact. This is due to the heavy pollution off the Belgian shore.

◆ *You can't beat a cold Belgian beer*

FISH & CHIPS BELGIAN STYLE

You don't have to spend a fortune to enjoy a good meal. The most famous and fast dish in the country is *moules frites*, which is typically a bowl of steamed mussels in either a clear, herbed broth or tomato-based sauce served up with crisp *frites* (French fries) and a dollop of mayonnaise. You can find this dish at almost every café and restaurant in the city – and each will keep their sauce ingredients a closely guarded secret.

Other seafood varieties to look out for include oysters, small, sweet-tasting shrimps from the North Sea and eels from the rural canals that dot the countryside. The spicy cocktail sauces and tartare sauces that are often served with British and American dishes aren't commonly served with Belgian fish and seafood, so if you really want the added condiments, you'll have to ask for them.

As for game and meat, these ingredients are best found in restaurants that specialise in cuisine from the Ardennes. The region's wild forests produce tasty venison, wild boar and pheasant. Rich flavours are this area's speciality, often to the detriment of simpler beef and chicken dishes. The shortage of large areas of grazing land means that beef isn't a speciality of Belgium, however, you will find it imported and on most menus.

World-famous Belgian beer washes the food down. There are about 120 breweries producing over 800 types of beer in a dozen styles with 50 subcategories available in Belgium.

USEFUL DINING PHRASES

I would like a table for ... people
Je voudrais une table pour ... personnes
Zher voodray ewn tabl poor ... pehrson

Waiter/waitress!
Monsieur/Mademoiselle,
s'il vous plaît
M'sewr/madmwahzel, sylvooplay

May I have the bill, please?
L'addition, s'il vous plaît.
Laddyssyawng, sylvooplay.

Does it have meat in it?
Est-ce que ce plat contient
de la viande?
*Essker ser plah kontyang
der lah veeahngd?*

Where is the toilet, please?
Où sont les toilettes,
s'il vous plaît?
*Oo sawng leh twahlaitt,
sylvooplay?*

A good café or restaurant will serve a minimum of ten different brands and varieties. Ask your bartender for a recommendation if you don't know which variety to try. You'll often find that beer is also an integral ingredient of the dish you are ordering for dinner. Note that some Belgian beers are very strong, with an alcohol content of 12 per cent.

❶ To help make your decisions, consider a day trip to nearby Leuven – home to the famous Stella Artois brewery. This massive factory offers tours of the facilities in addition to tastings of its product (see page 122).

Entertainment & nightlife

Brussels may be a hard-working town but it likes to play hard too. Locals think nothing of spending an evening sipping local brews in a bar, especially when they have such a variety of beers to choose from. City bars don't have an official closing time and many stay open until the wee hours of the morning. Take advantage of this situation by pulling up a bar stool and chatting to the locals who call these drinking dens their home from home. It is during these conversations that you truly capture the spirit of Brussels.

Cinema is another favourite pastime (films are usually shown in their original language, with subtitles). You can even see how the industry was built up during its early days at the fascinating Cinémathèque (see page 80), where there are regular nightly screenings of silent films complete with piano music accompaniment. Another popular option is **Kinepolis**, one of the world's biggest cinema complexes (ⓐ Bruparck ⓣ 02 474 2603 ⓦ www.kinepolis.com).

The city has a thriving local live music scene. It takes a lot for a local band to generate a following, as there are no laws that ensure Belgian bands will get airplay on local radio stations. There's everything from Jacques Brel-style *chanteurs* through to cutting-edge electro – but don't go expecting the selection of a London or even a Manchester. For big names, there are two large-scale venues that draw the crowds: The **Vorst Nationaal** (ⓐ Avenue Victor Rousseau 208, 1190 Forest ⓣ 0900 69500 ⓦ www.vorstnationaal.be) and the slightly more intimate **Ancienne Belgique** (ⓐ Avenue Anspachlaan 110 ⓣ 02 548 2424 ⓦ www.abconcerts.be).

⬤ An outdoor performance at the Brussels Jazz Marathon

As the home of the saxophone, Belgium is well known for its jazz venues. The now-ancient Toots Thielemans and the late great Django Reinhardt both cut their teeth in the clubs of Brussels. Join the throngs at the annual Jazz Marathon, which takes over hundreds of venues in the city every May (see page 10). It's a great opportunity to stroll from bar to bar and listen to performers both amateur and professional.

World music is another speciality of the city. A night in this happening community will expose you to African, Asian and South American sounds with a strong focus on the music of Belgium's former colony, the Congo. The biggest festival of world sounds is the Couleur Café festival in June at the **Tour & Taxis** (ⓐ Avenue du Port 86C ⓣ 02 424 2298 Ⓦ www.tourtaxis.be).

For a truly memorable evening, you should go clubbing. While the clubs of the capital aren't as 'wow' as those in the musically edgy cities of Antwerp or Leuven, there's still plenty to keep you occupied. The country considers itself to be the founding father of European techno and welcomes a plethora of international DJs to back up that claim.

The headquarters of this movement is the legendary club The Fuse (see page 70). At first glance you might find there isn't much to look at in this hangar-style space, but it's been at the forefront of musical styles for over a decade now and continues to welcome in the masses (even if there is more of a suburban vibe these days).

For the best nights out, avoid the branded clubs and go instead to the one-off nights at venues scattered throughout the city in alternative dance spaces. Recyclart (see page 70) is a great example of such an evening with its mission to showcase up-and-coming acts and DJs.

Sport & relaxation

PARTICIPATION SPORTS

Cycling

When it comes to keeping fit and exercising, Belgians are a hearty lot. Daily activity is a way of life for locals – and not simply due to a desire to keep the body trim and toned. Cycling and jogging are the most common methods of getting the heart pumping.

If you want to get on a bike to explore points in the city that are further afield, then it is possible to rent a bicycle on a daily or weekend rate. Prices start at around €13 for a day.

Pro Vélo ③ Rue de Londres 15 ❶ 02 502 7355 ⓦ www.provelo.org
🕒 10.00–18.00 Mon–Fri (Nov–Mar); 10.00–18.00 Mon–Fri, 13.00–14.00 Sat & Sun (Apr–Oct) Ⓜ Metro: Trône

Brussels now has a communal bike hire system. There are bike stations throughout the city, and you can buy a day or week ticket using a credit or debit card. The first 30 minutes are free.
ⓦ www.villo.be

Golf

Space limitations mean that large-scale athletic centres and golf courses are a rarity. Despite this, golf remains a popular pastime, with many Eurocrats using the links as an extension of their networking sessions. As the Eurocrats can spend, spend, spend, fees on local courses can be out of the affordable range for average tourists – especially during peak weekend periods. Phone ahead to determine costs and tee time possibilities.

A good bet for beginners is the Golf Club Academy and Training Centre close to the Fôret de Soignes, where you can book lessons

◑ *Ice-skating on the Grand Place*

from pros and training sessions. Contact the Academy for packages that include hotel rooms and multiple day passes if you want to make a full holiday out of your golfing experience.

Brabantse Golf Club ⓐ Steenwagenstraat 11, Melsbrook ⓣ 03 751 8205

Golf Club Academy and Training Centre ⓐ Chaussée de la Hulpe 53A ⓣ 02 672 2222 ⓦ www.brusselsgolfclub.com

Royal Golf Club of Belgium ⓐ Château de Ravenstein, Tervuren ⓣ 02 767 5801 ⓦ www.rgcb.be

Ice-skating

In winter ice-skating becomes the pastime of choice and there is no better (or more magical) place to enjoy it than in Sainte-Catherine. In the lead-up to Christmas, the Place du Marché-aux-Poissons becomes an outdoor skating rink where you can rent skates to glide past the historic architecture. Skates cost around €5 to rent. Combine it with a shopping trip at the Christmas market for a full seasonal experience.

Accommodation

Brussels has plenty of hotel rooms due to its function as the unofficial capital of the EU. While this means you can often find deals, it also puts a strong focus on business travelling needs – so some hotels are a bit lacking in character.

The basic rule of thumb is that properties in the Lower Town will be more expensive at weekends and designed for tourists, while hotels in the EU Quarter, outside the petite ceinture and close to the parliament buildings in Upper Town, will cater for those with large expense accounts.

Despite this wealth of accommodation, summers can get busy (especially at weekends), so if you are planning a visit around this time, it is best to book ahead.

If your visit to Brussels is a spur-of-the-moment decision, then consider booking your room through the **Brussels Tourist Information Office** (ⓐ Grand Place ❶ 02 513 8940 ⓦ www.brusselsinternational.be). Alternatively, book through **Resotel** (❶ 02 779 3939 ⓦ www.belgiumhospitality.com). Their rates can be very competitive.

PRICE CATEGORIES

Hotels in Belgium are graded according to a star system running from one star for a cheap guesthouse to five stars for a luxurious property with numerous facilities. The ratings in this book are per double or twin room per night.

£ up to €100   ££ €100–200   £££ over €200

HOTELS

Monty Hotel £–££ Inconveniently located but high on design sense, this great hotel features interior fittings from some of today's hottest designers (Philippe Starck, Ingo Maurer, etc.) and a welcoming atmosphere. Too bad it's so far from the city centre. Good for the sights at Parc du Cinquantenaire. ⓐ Boulevard Brand Whitlock 101 (Beyond the petite ceinture) ⓣ 02 734 5636 ⓦ www.monty-hotel.be ⓝ Metro: Montgomery

Café Pacific ££ Cool and hip, in one of Brussels' trendiest streets, this hotel also has a café-bar. The fashionable should love it, but maybe not those with more traditional tastes in hotel rooms. ⓐ Rue Antoine Dansaert 57 ⓣ 02 213 0080 ⓦ www.hotelcafepacific.com ⓝ Metro: Bourse

Noga ££ A nice choice if you want comfort on a budget. Noga offers colourful, clean rooms that are conveniently located for exploring the city. All rooms have en-suite showers. ⓐ Rue du Béguinage 38 (Lower Town) ⓣ 02 218 6763 ⓦ www.nogahotel.com ⓝ Metro: Sainte-Catherine

Stanhope ££–£££ If you can get a deal, this hotel is often a great place to rest your head. As the building comprises three classic town houses, there is a real home-from-home feel to the property. Rooms feature luxurious amenities such as marble bathrooms and canopied beds. Each room is different, so be sure to look at a few options before you make your final selection. ⓐ Rue du Commerce 9 (Beyond the petite ceinture) ⓣ 02 506 9111 ⓦ www.stanhope.be ⓝ Metro: Trône

◔ Hotel Amigo offers luxury in the heart of the city

Hotel Amigo £££ Check in here if you truly want to impress the one you're with. Once a prison, the Amigo is now the hottest spot in town for visiting celebs and minor royals. Acres of marble, the finest silks, crisp linens – it's all here in abundance. Service is uniformly spectacular. Magritte and Tintin prints in the rooms add a Belgian touch. ⓐ Rue de l'Amigo 1–3 (Lower Town) ⓣ 02 547 4747 ⓦ www.hotelamigo.com ⓝ Metro: Gare Centrale

Radisson Blu Royal £££ Great location, not far from the Grand Place, this is one of Brussels' best hotels, popular with both business and leisure travellers. It has many facilities such as a health club and parking. The foyer atrium is something to behold. The hotel's fish restaurant is one of the best in town. ⓐ Rue du Fossé-aux-Loups 47 ⓣ 02 227 3040 ⓦ www.radissonblu.com ⓝ Metro: De Brouckère

GUESTHOUSES & B&BS

La Vieille Lanterne £ Small family-run B&B overlooking the Manneken Pis. Each of the six rooms has an en-suite shower. Furnishings are basic but clean – and you can't beat the breakfast in bed included in the room price. ⓐ Rue des Grands Carmes 29 (Lower Town) ⓣ 02 512 7494 ⓦ www.lavieillelanterne.be ⓝ Metro: Bourse

Vaudeville B&B £–££ The Vaudeville has only four elegant rooms, but the extraordinary location is the thing here: this B&B is actually in the Galeries Royales Saint-Hubert, above the Vaudeville café (where you have breakfast). It can be noisy for those who like to turn in early, but otherwise an unusual

experience. ⓐ Galerie de la Reine 11 ☎ 02 511 2345
🌐 www.chambresdhotesduvaudeville.be
Ⓜ Metro: Gare Centrale

HOSTELS

Centre Vincent Van Gogh £ This massive youth hostel is the
largest cheap sleep option in town. Often busy with school
groups, it can become fully booked months in advance. Well
stocked with games and bright common rooms, it's a clean
and simple place to rest your head – so long as you don't
mind sharing with gaggles of pre-teens on a class trip.
ⓐ Rue Traversière 8 (Beyond the petite ceinture) ☎ 02 217 0158
🌐 www.chab.be Ⓜ Metro: Botanique

Sleep Well £ Bright and friendly youth hostel with great
transport links. Singles, doubles, triples and dorms are on offer.
Bathrooms are shared. Sheets cost extra. Spend a little more for
a room in the Star section if you want the luxury of an en-suite
bathroom. ⓐ Rue du Damier 23 (Lower Town) ☎ 02 218 5050
🌐 www.sleepwell.be Ⓜ Metro: Rogier

THE BEST OF BRUSSELS

Brussels offers much to entertain, interest and please the senses, and is a great place to visit for a short weekend break filled with fine art, chocolate and beer.

TOP 10 ATTRACTIONS

- **Grand Place** Brussels' main square, described by Victor Hugo as the most beautiful square in Europe (see page 59).

- **Manneken Pis** He may just be a boy having a wee, but to many he's the symbol of a nation (see page 62).

- **Musée Horta** A graceful example of the contribution to Art Nouveau made by Belgium's favourite architect (see page 95).

- **Atomium** This super-size model of an atom remains a popular tourist destination. The views from the top are superb (see page 86).

- **Parc du Cinquantenaire** The city's favourite green space, built by Léopold II (see page 90).

- **Musées Royaux des Beaux-Arts** Choose from the Flemish Primitives in the Ancient wing, contemporary works in the Modern collection, or the Magritte Museum (see page 81).

- **Musée du Cacao et du Chocolat** Sweet, sinful and oh so delicious. The museum dedicated to its development is worth sinking your teeth into (see page 65).

- **Toone** Much-loved puppet theatre with outlandishly satirical shows performed by highly detailed marionettes (see page 71).

- **Centre Belge de la Bande Dessinée** In the land of Tintin and Hergé, don't miss this excellent collection of contemporary comic strips (see page 58).

- **Beer, glorious beer** Brussels is the city to go to for the widest selection of beer (see page 71).

The fascinating Musées Royaux des Beaux-Arts

Suggested itineraries

HALF-DAY: BRUSSELS IN A HURRY

Head straight for the Grand Place (see page 59) and explore the guild houses that line this lovely square. From here, join a tour of the historic Hôtel de Ville (see page 59) and then grab some *frites* from one of the nearby vendors.

1 DAY: TIME TO SEE A LITTLE MORE

Begin your visit by taking in the beauty of the Grand Place. Head south out of the square to visit the Manneken Pis (see page 62) – you'll know you're there when you spot the crowds. Have lunch in a local café and then head over to Lower Town to enjoy the shopping opportunities, making sure you don't miss Les Galeries Royales Saint-Hubert arcade (see page 22) with its luxury boutiques.

2–3 DAYS: TIME TO SEE MUCH MORE

Two or three days is the average length of a stay in Brussels, and there is much you can do to make the most of your time. Pack your first day with the suggestions above and then head straight to Upper Town on the morning of your second day. Here is where you'll find the best art galleries and museums in the city.

LONGER: ENJOYING BRUSSELS TO THE FULL

To experience all that Brussels has to offer, you need to go beyond the petite ceinture. Spend a day in Ixelles for colourful African culture and unique boutiques. Visit the EU Quarter to understand the inner workings of the European Parliament, and end your day by watching the sunset from the Atomium (see page 86).

⬥ *Don't fight the temptation – make the time to indulge*

Something for nothing

On a budget? Never fear. You don't need to break the bank to have a good time in Brussels. Most of the city's finest sights are absolutely free. Even a tasty snack only costs a euro or two if you know where to look.

The Grand Place is the heart of the city and a stop to admire the architecture won't even cost you the fluff in your pocket. The guild houses that surround the square showcase the Golden Age of the city when merchants ruled the nation. While each house is unique, they all come together in a satisfying swirl with a heavy Italian Baroque influence.

Manneken Pis (see page 62), the symbol of the city, is also free of charge and just a few steps south of the square on Rue de l'Etuve. It may shock you when you see the famous peeing boy, as the fountain is a lot smaller than you would expect. Gates surround the Manneken Pis to protect him from graffiti and protesters. Luckily, he is mounted on a pedestal to give tourists greater viewing opportunities.

Churches are another source of affordable tourist possibilities. The city's places of worship are particularly fascinating due to the number of battles between Catholics and Protestants that were fought during the troubled Reformation and Counter-Reformation periods. Some of the more intriguing churches include four of the city's six Notre-Dames: Bon-Secours, de la Chapelle, du Finistère, and aux Riches Claires (see page 63).

The great outdoors is well loved by residents and there are plenty of glorious parks in which to enjoy a day strolling through the shaded lawns. The most interesting is the Parc du

Cinquantenaire (see page 90). King Léopold II had the park built in order to commemorate the 50th anniversary of the founding of the Belgian nation. These days it is surrounded by a number of cultural institutions allowing visitors to combine a walk in the woods with a bit of inspiring art and architecture.

🔺 *Visit many interesting churches for free*

When it rains

Upper Town is the place to go when the rain comes tumbling down – and in Brussels you can be pretty sure that this will happen at least once during your visit. The Upper Town neighbourhood is a great location to kill a few hours because of its collection of large museums and galleries, particularly the combined Musée d'Art Ancien (see page 82), the Musée d'Art Moderne (see page 82) and the Magritte Museum (see page 81).

If these galleries don't take your fancy, there are plenty of other options in the immediate vicinity, including the Palais Royal (see page 78), Palais Coudenberg (see page 78), BELvue (see page 80) and the Musée des Instruments de Musique (see page 81).

With children in tow, the last of these is the best of the bunch, as little ones may get a little tired of wandering through historical room after historical room. Alternatively, take them to the Cinémathèque (see page 80), where you can watch a silent film from the early days of cinema complete with piano accompaniment.

Another great option if you want to stick close to the Grand Place is the Scientastic Museum (see page 131). Children and adults alike love the interactive displays that explore the wonders of science. Factsheets are available in English.

Finally, if you plan ahead, try to book tickets to see the show at the Toone puppet theatre (see page 71). Eight generations of puppet masters from the same family have built this company into a national treasure. Be warned, performances here are heavy on satire and conducted mostly in a strange local dialect.

But while many of the jokes will go over your head, you'll appreciate the artistry of the puppets and attention to detail.

If all else fails and you're desperate to do some damage to your wallet, head to a *galerie*. There are a few of these covered shopping walkways dotted in and around the petite ceinture, of which Les Galeries Royales Saint-Hubert (see page 22) is the best known. Here is where you will find exclusive boutiques and high-end wares suitable for primo souvenir hunters.

▲ *Les Galeries Royales Saint-Hubert is an excellent place to avoid the weather*

On arrival

TIME DIFFERENCE

Belgian clocks follow Central European Time (CET). During Daylight Saving Time (end Mar–end Oct), the clocks are put forward one hour.

ARRIVING

By air

Most air travellers to Brussels will arrive at Zaventem International Airport. There are several scheduled airlines that currently fly into the airport, with services from many UK regional departure points. Charleroi Airport is the airport of choice for Ryanair, located an inconvenient 55 km (34 miles) from the city centre.

To get to the city centre from Zaventem Airport, take the Airport City Express train service for the 20-minute journey. Four departures per hour make the journey between 06.00 and 24.00. Tickets cost around €3 one way. From Charleroi, board public bus number 68 and connect to the half-hourly train from Charleroi Station to Brussels. The journey time is approximately one hour.

Charleroi Airport ✆ 07 125 1211 ⓦ www.charleroi-airport.com
Zaventem Airport ✆ 090 070 000 ⓦ www.brusselsairport.be
Airport City Express Train ✆ 02 528 2828 ⓦ www.b-rail.be
British Airways ✆ 0844 493 0787 ⓦ www.ba.com
Brussels Airlines ✆ 0905 60 95 609
ⓦ www.brusselsairlines.com
Ryanair ⓦ www.ryanair.com

By rail

Eurostar trains from the UK arrive at the Gare du Midi, southwest of the city centre. Check-in for trains on the return journey needs to be completed a minimum of 20 minutes before departure. Journey time to and from London St Pancras International is approximately two hours. From most other points in Europe, trains also terminate at Gare du Midi. Some stop at Gare Centrale (slightly east of the centre) en route.

By road

Belgium is an easy country to drive in. Streets are well marked and well lit, and the motorway system is fast, efficient and extensive. From the coast and ferries bringing visitors from the UK, take the E40/A10 straight to the city via Ghent. Alternatively, take the E19 south from the Netherlands, or follow the E314/A2

⬤ *Gare Centrale is very near the Grand Place*

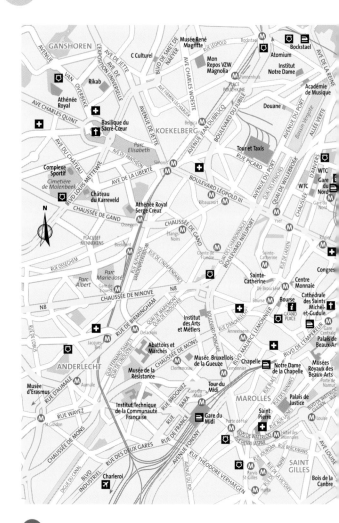

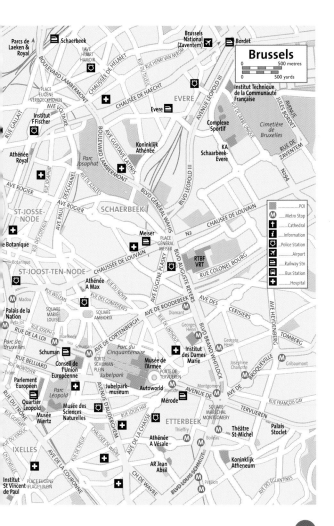

through the Netherlands from Germany. Once you reach the ring road that circles the city, it is relatively easy to get into the centre by following the motorway signs. Parking is available both on-street and in car parks. Consider selecting a hotel with parking if you plan on bringing your car, as daily rates can add up.

FINDING YOUR FEET

Brussels is a large city of individual neighbourhoods. When exploring specific districts, walking is the best option. For travel between districts, the extensive metro, bus and tram systems are incredibly efficient. Metro trains run regularly and whizz visitors off to almost every corner of the city.

ORIENTATION

Brussels is an extremely easy city to navigate in terms of neighbourhood locations, but difficult once you get to street level. In the city centre, streets are compact, cobbled and wind in all sorts of directions.

One easy way to keep track of your location is to remember that the Centre Monnaie is essentially the main intersection of Lower Town, while the Grand Place and the Gare Centrale act as the bridge into Upper Town, with the Parc de Bruxelles lying at the heart of the Upper Town district.

A circle of boulevards known as the petite ceinture runs around the city centre, effectively separating it from the outlying districts. Travellers visiting Brussels will most likely base themselves somewhere within the petite ceinture unless they are visiting on business, when a location in the EU Quarter might prove more convenient.

IF YOU GET LOST, TRY ...

Do you speak English?
Parlez-vous anglais?
Pahrlayvoo ahnglay?

Is this the way to...?
C'est la bonne direction pour...?
Seh lah bon deereekseeawng poor...?

Can you point to it on my map?
Pouvez-vous me le montrer sur la carte?
Poovehvoo mer ler mawngtreh sewr lah kart?

If you travel by Eurostar, you will arrive at the Gare du Midi, to the southwest of the city centre. From the Gare du Midi, it's just a short metro hop to the sights, hotels and cafés of the Lower Town.

GETTING AROUND

An integrated tram, metro and bus system operated by the **STIB/MIVB** (☎ 02 515 2000 ⓦ www.stib.be) can take you to pretty much every point in the city you might want to visit. Metro trains and trams start running at 05.30 and finish at 24.00. Tickets for all the listed methods of transport can be purchased from metro and rail stations, newsagents, tourist information centres, and on buses and trains. Single tickets valid for a one-hour journey cost from around €1.70 (€2 if purchased on a vehicle), while day passes good for unlimited travel are about €4. Alternatively, purchase a *carnet* (or 'book') of ten tickets for around €9.80 or a Brussels Card designed for tourists

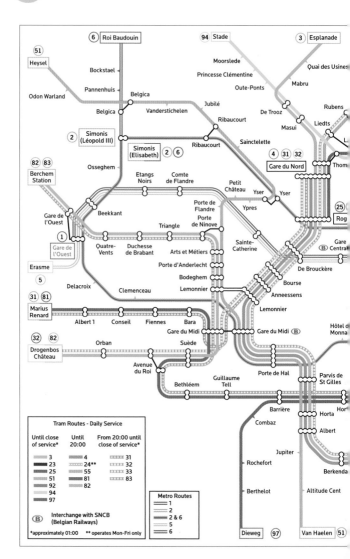

that offers up to three days of unlimited public transport and admission to 25 museums for €40. Children under six travelling with an adult who has purchased the card travel free. You can also buy 24- and 48-hour cards (€24 and €34).

CAR HIRE

If you are planning a trip out to Antwerp, Ghent or somewhere further afield, you may want to hire a car.

❶ Rates vary according to season and length of hire, but special offers are available – check the Internet.

❶ The minimum age for hiring an economy car is 21.

Avis ⓐ Gare du Midi, Rue de France 2 ❶ 02 527 1705
ⓦ www.avis.be ⓛ 08.00–18.00 Mon–Fri ⓝ Metro: Gare du Midi
Budget ⓐ Avenue Louise 327B ❶ 02 646 5130 ⓦ www.budget.be
ⓛ 08.00–18.00 Mon–Fri, 09.00–12.00 Sat ⓝ Metro: Louise
Hertz ⓐ Boulevard Maurice Lemonnier 8 ❶ 02 513 2886
ⓦ www.hertz.be ⓛ 08.30–17.00 Mon–Fri, 08.00–14.00 Sat, 09.00–13.00 Sun ⓝ Metro: Anneessens

◗ *The clock at Mont des Arts*

THE CITY OF
Brussels

Lower Town

When you think of Belgium, the sights you most associate with the country can all be found in the winding streets of Brussels' Lower Town. Here is where the Manneken Pis piddles away to the delight of his thousands of daily admirers, where the grace and elegance of the Grand Place seduces fans of architecture, and where boutiques peek out from walls of ancient buildings enticing visitors with their displays of lace and mouthwatering chocolate.

Also included in Lower Town's 'borders' is the historical heart of the district, St-Géry, which is where the first buildings of the city were constructed centuries ago, as well as the ancient port area of Sainte-Catherine, now known for its seafood restaurants.

Finally, in the southeast corner of Lower Town is Les Marolles, a working-class district with a strong sense of community that battles every day against encroaching gentrification.

SIGHTS & ATTRACTIONS

Centre Belge de la Bande Dessinée

Belgians love humour and art. So it should come as no surprise that there is a museum dedicated to the art of the comic strip. While the work of Hergé and the story of Tintin make up a large section of the collection, there's plenty more than just images of Snowy to stare at. ⓐ Rue des Sables 20 ⓣ 02 219 1980 ⓦ www.comicscenter.net ⓛ 10.00–18.00 Tues–Sun ⓝ Metro: Rogier ⓘ Admission charge. Be warned: this museum is a cerebral examination of the comic and not designed with children in mind.

Grand Place & Hôtel de Ville

Once described by Victor Hugo as the most beautiful square in the world, the Grand Place is the spiritual heart of the city. Now given UNESCO World Heritage Site status, it is the most visited spot in Brussels – and for good reason.

The Grand Place developed its distinctive look thanks to the influential city guilds. The guilds craved power. In order to achieve this, they needed two things: a strong base and proximity to the Hôtel de Ville. As each guild grew in prominence, they built or branded homes close to the Hôtel de Ville and added markings to signify their status. Therefore, a statue of the patron saint of tallow dealers exists outside their

⬤ *An ornate fountain embellishes the inner courtyard of the Hôtel de Ville*

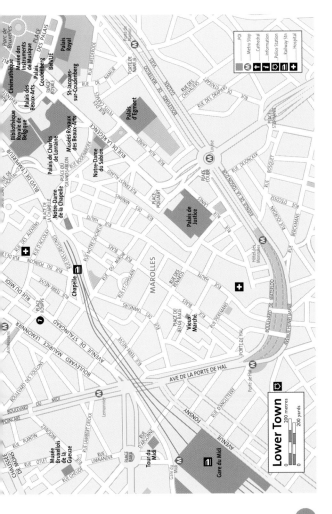

Lower Town

POI
Metro Stop
Cathedral
Information
Police Station
Railway Stn
Hospital

Parc de Bruxelles
PLACE DES PALAIS
Palais Royal
Cinémathèque
Musée des Instruments de Musique
Palais des Beaux-Arts
PLACE ROYALE
Palais Coudenberg
BELVUE
Bellevue
St-Jacques-sur-Coudenberg
Bibliothèque Royale de Belgique
Palais de Charles de Lorraine
Musées Royaux des Beaux-Arts
Palais d'Egmont
Notre-Dame du Sablon
PLACE DU GRAND SABLON
RUE DE LA RÉGENCE
Notre-Dame de la Chapelle
PLACE JEU DE BALLE
Palais de Justice
Chapelle
MAROLLES
Vieux Marché
PLACE DU JEU DE BALLE
RUE DU MIDI
BOULEVARD MAURICE LEMONNIER
AVENUE DE STALINGRAD
PORTE DE HAL
AVE DE LA PORTE DE HAL
Musée Bruxellois de la Gueuze
Tour du Midi
Gare du Midi
FONSNY
AVENUE

0 200 metres
0 200 yards

former guild house, while the detail of a hop plant is carved above the door to the brewers' guild. Some of the more noteworthy guild houses include the haberdashers' guild house, the brewers' guild house and the artists' guild.

What makes the Grand Place so special is the architecture. The plots of land that the houses lie on are extremely small, giving grace and elegance to the compact yet ornate Italian Baroque style. The crowning glory is the Hôtel de Ville, built in the early 15th century. This amazing building took 50 years to build with ornate wings, a belfry and a 113 m (371 ft) tower with a gilded statue of St Michael slaying the Devil at the very top. You'll note that the left wing may seem smaller than the right. This is not a mistake. Rather, it was a conscious decision made in order to accommodate the existing street grid pattern. A guided tour taking visitors through the beautiful official rooms is highly recommended. However, visitors are not permitted in the tower.

Hôtel de Ville Ⓐ Grand Place Ⓣ 02 279 4343 Ⓛ Guided tours in English 15.15 Tues & Wed (Apr–Sept); 10.45 & 12.15 Sun (year-round) Ⓝ Metro: Bourse

Manneken Pis

Belgium's national symbol is actually a lot smaller than you might expect. Always surrounded by crowds, the fountain is now blocked off by gated railings to protect him from admirers. On special days, he is costumed to reflect the season. Look for the nearby framed sign to see when he is next set to don a colourful outfit. Try to go early in the day or late in the afternoon for the best view. Ⓐ Rue de l'Etuve Ⓝ Metro: Bourse/Gare Centrale

Notre-Dame de Bon-Secours

For an example of Flemish Renaissance architecture, look
no further than this Baroque church built in the late 1600s –
widely considered to be the most beautiful in the district.
ⓐ Rue du Marché-au-Charbon ⓣ 02 514 3113 ⓛ 09.00–17.00
daily (winter); 09.00–18.00 daily (summer)
Ⓝ Metro: Anneessens

Notre-Dame de la Chapelle

This is the ultimate mishmash of a building. The original chapel
was built in the 12th century; the nave is 15th-century Gothic;
and the art collection is largely 19th century. It is the burial
place of civil rights campaigner François Anneessens and of
Pieter Brueghel the Elder and his wife. ⓐ Place de la Chapelle
ⓣ 02 512 2140 ⓛ daily 09.00–19.00 Ⓝ Metro: Anneessens

Notre-Dame du Finistère

Once the site of a 15th-century chapel, the present church was
built on top of the existing structure in the early 18th century.
The most noteworthy feature is the wildly Baroque pulpit.
ⓐ Rue Neuve ⓣ 02 217 5252 ⓛ 08.00–18.00 Mon–Sat,
08.00–12.00, 15.00–18.00 Sun Ⓝ Metro: De Brouckère/Rogier

Notre-Dame aux Riches Claires

It is believed that this church was designed and built in 1665
by a student of Rubens named Luc Fayd'herbe. Renovations
re-energised the structure in 2000. ⓐ Rue des Riches Claires 23
ⓣ 02 511 5099 ⓛ 16.00–18.00 Sat, 09.30–14.00 Sun
Ⓝ Metro: Bourse

Sainte-Catherine Church

This church has experienced a wealth of history and has a number of unsavoury features, including a purpose-built *pissoir* (public urinal) constructed in between its buttresses. Unloved by the local populace, it was almost transformed into the city's stock exchange before opening its doors to its congregation in 1867. Today, it is a graceful house of worship filled with stained-glass windows and minor art treasures. ⓐ Place Sainte-Catherine ⓣ 02 513 3481 ⓞ 08.30–17.00 Mon–Sat, 09.00–12.00 Sun ⓜ Metro: Sainte-Catherine

🔺 *The brewing museum is housed in the Maison des Brasseurs Belges*

St-Jean-Baptiste au Béguinage Church

Another example of Flemish Baroque architecture, this church features a warm amber-hued façade and a collection of 17th-century paintings by Theodoor van Loon. Place du Béguinage 02 217 8742 daily 09.00–17.00 Metro: Sainte-Catherine

St-Nicholas Church

This elegant church was founded in the 11th century and features a moody Gothic interior that has recently undergone extensive renovation. The curves of the walls follow the old course of the River Senne. Rue au Beurre 1 02 513 8022 14.00–17.00 Mon, 10.00–17.00 Tues–Sat, 13.00–17.00 Sun Metro: Bourse

CULTURE

Musée des Brasseurs Belges

This museum has a permanent collection that examines both ancient and modern methods of brewing beer. Grand Place 10 02 511 4987 daily 10.00–17.00 (summer); 10.00–16.30 Mon–Fri, 12.00–16.30 Sat & Sun (winter) Metro: Bourse Admission charge

Musée du Cacao et du Chocolat

Chocolate was introduced to the world by the Aztecs and this museum examines the journey the sweet stuff has taken since that time. Seminal moments include the development of praline and the history of the industry in Belgium. Rue de la Tête d'Or 9/11 02 514 2048 www.mucc.be 10.30–16.30

Tues–Sun (Sept–June); 10.00–17.00 daily (July & Aug) Metro:
Bourse Admission charge

Musée de la Ville de Bruxelles

When this building was constructed in the 13th century it was
known as the Broodhuis (or 'Bread House'), as it was owned
by the bakers' guild. Today, it holds the museum of the city of
Brussels. Collections include some rather faded tapestries,
but it's the wardrobe of more than 600 costumes designed
for the Manneken Pis and some delightful Breughel paintings
that really draw the crowds. Grand Place 02 279 4350
www.brucity.be 10.00–17.00 Tues–Sun Metro:
Bourse/Gare Centrale Admission charge

RETAIL THERAPY

In Lower Town, the streets around the Grand Place and the
Manneken Pis are chock-full of Belgian tourist tat, including cut-rate
chocolatiers, 'Made in China' lace shops and boutiques
celebrating the EU government. For something a little more
authentic, go instead to the Rue des Eperonniers southeast
of the square.

Glamour can be added to your life in the form of the shops of
Les Galeries Royales Saint-Hubert (see page 22), a famous
shopping arcade opened in 1847 that is home to a collection of
boutiques selling handmade and well-crafted clothing,
accessories, hats and lace.

High-street labels can be found on the Rue Neuve – the
Oxford Street or Fifth Avenue of Brussels. Here is where you

will come across well-known European labels such as Benetton, Zara and H&M. The northern end of the street also boasts City 2, a large shopping centre, and a branch of the Inno department store. If the crowds start to get on your nerves, get off the street and head instead to the unique boutiques and independent shops of the Rue des Fripiers or Rue du Marché aux Herbes.

Better yet, if unique and independent really are what you prefer when you're digging out your wallet, head down to the neighbourhoods of Sainte-Catherine and St-Géry. The Rue Antoine Dansaert is shopping central for street wear, quirky gifts, and cutting-edge design and furnishings. Young designers often make this their first stop when looking for locations to build their boutiques.

Vieux Marché

One person's junk is another's treasure at this flea market located in a vibrant immigrant neighbourhood. If you lack the patience to rummage through everything on display, go instead to the antique shops that line Rue Blaes and Rue Haute. Be aware of your wallets and purses if you do decide to visit, as the Les Marolles district (where the market is situated) has a reputation for petty theft. ⓐ Place du Jeu de Balle ⓝ Metro: Porte de Hal

TAKING A BREAK

Chéz Leon £ ❶ If you have the children in tow but want to try some cracking Belgian cuisine, then this buzzy restaurant should fit the bill. The paper napkins and photographed menus give the place a fast-food feel, but that shouldn't dissuade you from trying the delicious local favourites such as *moules frites* (mussels and chips). There's pushchair parking here and children under 12 get a free set menu when accompanied by a paying adult. ⓐ Rue des Bouchers 18 ⓣ 02 511 1415 ⓦ www.chezleon.be ⓛ 12.00–23.00 daily ⓜ Metro: Bourse

Bij den Boer ££ ❷ It isn't pretty, but this greasy-spoon style establishment dishes up stunning pots of mussels and thick, rich *bouillabaisse*. Service isn't great – and there is no point complaining – but you won't be rushed when you finally do get your food. A great place for a lazy winter afternoon. ⓐ Quai aux Briques 60 ⓣ 02 512 6122 ⓦ www.bijdenboer.com ⓛ 12.00–14.30, 18.00–22.30 Mon–Sat ⓜ Metro: Sainte-Catherine

AFTER DARK

RESTAURANTS
Belga Queen ££ ❸ All Belgian – all the time. That's what this restaurant is famous for. From the interiors to the food to the hinges on the doors – everything is made in Belgium and all the fresher for it. Once a bank, its large ceilings and imposing look make it more of a place for groups than romancing couples. ⓐ Rue du Fossé aux Loups 32 ⓣ 02 217 2187 ⓦ www.belgaqueen.be ⓛ 12.00–14.30, 19.00–24.00 daily ⓜ Metro: De Brouckère

Bonsoir Clara ££ ❹ Chic and appealing restaurant with creative modern cuisine and friendly service. ⓐ Rue Antoine Dansaert

22–26 ☎ 02 502 0990 ⏱ 12.00–14.30, 19.00–23.30 Mon–Thur,
12.00–14.30 Fri, 19.00–24.00 Sat & Sun Ⓝ Metro: Sainte-Catherine

Taverne du Passage ££ ❺ A very popular local institution, in the
Galeries Royales Saint-Hubert, specialising in Belgian cuisine
served by uniformed waiters. ⓐ Galerie de la Reine 30 ☎ 02 512
3731 ⓦ www.tavernedupassage.com ⏱ 12.00–24.00 daily
(Aug–May); closed Wed & Thur (June & July)

Viva M'Boma ££ ❻ In an old tripe shop, and specialising in offal,
but there is also much other excellent Belgian food worth
eating. Try for a table in the garden. ⓐ Rue de Flandre 17 ☎ 02 512
1593 Ⓝ Metro: Sainte-Catherine

Comme Chez Soi £££ ❼ Considered by many to be the best
restaurant in the country, this intimate eatery features fine Art
Nouveau interiors and inventive menus. The house speciality of
fillet of sole with white mousseline and shrimps is never dropped
from the always-changing bill of fare. Delicate blossoms should be
warned that ventilation is poor. ⓐ Place Rouppe 23 ☎ 02 512 2921
ⓦ www.commechezsoi.be ⏱ 12.00–14.15, 19.00–23.00 Tues &
Thur–Sat, 19.00–23.00 Wed Ⓝ Metro: Anneessens

BARS & NIGHTCLUBS

L'Archiduc Going since 1937, this Art Deco bar, on two floors, is
a favourite of locals in one of Brussels' coolest streets. It was
once famous for live jazz, which is now restricted to early
evenings at weekends. ⓐ Rue Antoine Dansaert 6 ☎ 02 512 0652
ⓦ www.archiduc.net ⏱ 16.00–05.00 daily Ⓝ Metro: Bourse

Bar Soixante This replaced the very successful Pablo Discobar. If you like Techno, Electrohouse and Drum & Bass, you should visit. Its atmosphere is bright and friendly and its doors open free of charge. Rue du Marché aux Charbon 02 514 5149 21.00–late Wed–Sun Metro: Bourse

The Fuse More than 2,000 clubbers pack into this superclub, which is heavy on international DJs and light on interiors. Expect deep house and up-for-it crowds. Rue Blaes 208 02 511 9789 www.fuse.be 22.00–05.00 Thur, 22.00–07.00 Fri & Sat Metro: Porte de Hal/Gare du Midi

Recyclart New talent is the mainstay of this electronic venue. Built as part of an urban regeneration project, it features tomorrow's big names today. When it's good, it's really, really good. But when it's bad, it's awful. Go with no expectations and you're likely to have the best night of your stay. Gare de Bruxelles-Chapelle, Rue des Ursulines 02 502 5734 www.recyclart.be Opening times vary Metro: Gare Centrale

CINEMAS & THEATRES
Théâtre National This national theatre caters for the French-speaking community of Belgium. Programming includes everything from new works by local playwrights to old classics produced with a contemporary edge. Boulevard Emile Jacqmain 111–115 02 203 5303 www.theatrenational.be Box office: 10.00–18.00 Mon–Fri Metro: Rogier

Toone The Toone puppet theatre has passed through the same family for eight generations and continues to produce riotous puppet shows to sell-out crowds. There are now more than 1,300 puppets, with new ones being prepared every year as public figures gain prominence. ⓐ Petite Rue des Bouchers 21 ⓣ 02 513 5486 ⓦ www.toone.be ⓛ Hours and performance times vary ⓜ Metro: Bourse/Gare Centrale

⬤ *The agonising dilemma of having to choose (see next page)*

KNOWING YOUR BEER

When it comes to beer, the bottles brewed in Belgium are considered by most to be the finest in the world. There is a brew to suit every occasion, taste and meal – and locals are wont to be extremely choosy when selecting their drink of choice.

While beer owes its origins to the Middle East more than 10,000 years ago, it was the Romans who popularised the drink in Western Europe around the 5th century. Monks had a monopoly on brewing and used the profits to maintain their brewing facilities.

When the Middle Ages arrived, the guilds took control of the industry and the number of breweries increased hugely. By the 16th century beer and ale were staples of society and profits were huge.

At its peak in 1900, there were more than 3,000 breweries in the country. Unfortunately, two world wars, the Great Depression and the popularisation of the cocktail culture have reduced that number to about 100. Does this mean that beer-making in Belgium is over? On the contrary, it has ensured that only the finest breweries have survived, and drinking the golden-hued liquid is more popular than ever.

While there are few breweries in Brussels, the city is the best place to plan a beer-tasting tour as the bars offer the widest selection of bottles from the most breweries. The beer museum on the Grand Place, the Musée des

Brasseurs Belges (see page 65), is a good place to go for a brief overview of the industry, with a day trip to Leuven an absolute must if you want to challenge your taste buds further.

When embarking on a tasting session at a Belgian bar, you'll find that a typical establishment will usually have on tap a draught lager such as Stella Artois or Maes and a wheat beer such as Hoegaarden. Wheat beer is generally considered to be more of a summer drink and is usually served in large tankards. A better bar will expand on this selection with offerings from smaller and more obscure breweries.

The Holy Grail of beers is the Trappist varieties produced by Trappist monks in the towns of Chimay, Westmalle, Orval, Rochefort and Westvleteren. These beers are for the pros and pack a killer alcoholic kick. A standard variety will be dark brown and creamy. However, there are double and triple versions that are even stronger, darker and creamier.

Other unique brews are Lambics (which are naturally fermented without the use of yeast and often developed in the Brussels area), Gueuze (which mixes older and younger versions of Lambic for an acquired taste) and fruit beers (which range from ultra tart to sweet).

If you're looking to bring a few bottles of your favourite find back home, it is possible to arrange shipping. Alternatively, stock up at any supermarket.

Upper Town

Situated on the top of a hill, Brussels' Upper Town was created on the orders of King Lambert II who wanted to move the royal family away from the murky and smelly waters of the River Senne. Nobles and wealthy merchants followed and transformed the area into the neighbourhood that can be seen today – a collection of palaces, parks, museums and government buildings ripe for exploration. But if that doesn't entice, the elegant shopping and supping in Sablon should. An evening in this elegant square will make you feel like a king.

SIGHTS & ATTRACTIONS

Cathédrale des Saints-Michel-et-Gudule

Since its completion, this church dedicated to the male and female patron saints of the city has survived graffiti attacks by Protestants and looting by French Revolutionary forces. Today it is a symbol of the city due to its glorious stained-glass windows and 11th-century Romanesque crypt. ⓐ Place Ste Gudule ❶ 02 217 8345 ⓦ www.cathedralestmichel.be ❶ 08.00–18.00 Mon–Fri, 08.30–18.00 Sat & Sun Ⓜ Metro: Gare Centrale ❶ Admission charge

Notre-Dame du Sablon

Having emerged from a recent renovation, this church was built to accommodate a statue of Mary shipped in from Antwerp that allegedly had healing powers. Unfortunately, the statue was destroyed by Protestants during the Iconoclastic Riots in the

16th century. The statue's arrival continues to be celebrated every July during Ommegang celebrations. See page 12 for details of this citywide festival. ⓐ Rue de la Régence 3B ⓘ 02 511 5741 ⓛ 09.00–18.30 Mon–Sat Ⓜ Metro: Porte de Namur

⬥ The impressive Cathédrale des Saints-Michel-et-Gudule

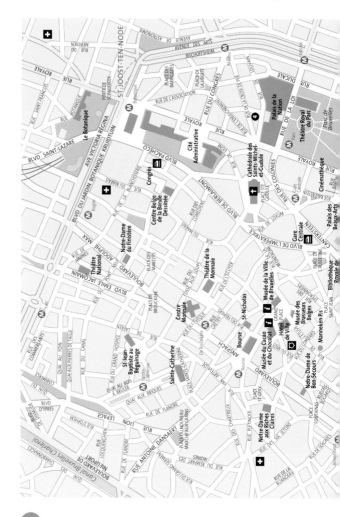

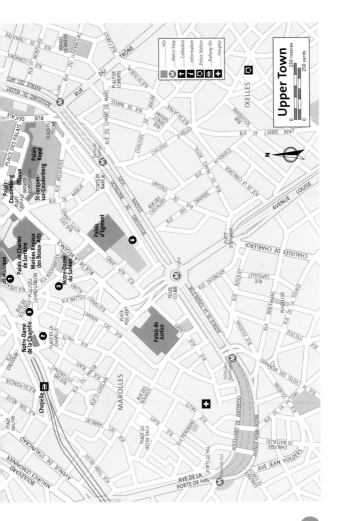

Upper Town

POI
Metro Stop
Cathedral
Information
Police Station
Railway Str
Hospital

0 250 metres
0 250 yards

IXELLES

MAROLLES

Palais Coudenberg
Bellevue
St-Jacques-sur-Coudenberg
Palais Royal
Palais de Charles de Lorraine
Musées Royaux des Beaux-Arts
Palais d'Egmont
Notre-Dame du Sablon
Notre-Dame de la Chapelle
Palais de Justice

77

Palais Coudenberg

Step back in time by exploring the excavated remains of the former palace of Belgium's nobility. Destroyed by a devastating fire in 1731, the palace was never rebuilt – but recent archaeological work has uncovered the remains of some of the rooms. The streets surrounding the remains date back to the same period and are just as fascinating as the site itself. Place des Palais 7 070 22 04 92 www.coudenberg.com 10.00–17.00 Tues–Fri, 10.00–18.00 Sat & Sun Metro: Parc Admission charge

Palais de Justice

More than 3,000 houses were razed to build this massive palace for Léopold II, which drove the architect mad during the course of the project's completion. No one can quite agree what style the palace was built in, but the symmetry is perfect and incredibly imposing. If you have to choose one palace to visit, make this the one. Place Poelaert 02 508 6111 08.00–17.00 Mon–Fri Metro: Louise

Palais Royal

This residential palace lacks the charm of some of the other stately homes of the city and features a mishmash of architectural styles due to a near-constant policy of remodelling begun in 1825. Place des Palais 02 551 2020 www.monarchie.be Hours vary, Tues–Sun late July–late Sept Metro: Trône

Place Royale

Built on the ruins of the palace of the Dukes of Brabant, this elegant square possesses beautiful examples of neoclassical architecture in the heart of the city's Upper Town. The Grand Place and Lower Town may have been the focus of power during the 17th and 18th centuries, but the Austrian overlords moved government to this locale during their period of rule. Restoration

◔ *The imposing interior of the Palais de Justice*

of the buildings is ongoing, so don't be surprised if some of the façades are covered with scaffolding. Trams: 92, 93, 94

St-Jacques-sur-Coudenberg

Built to look like a Roman temple in 1775, this church possesses an ancient resemblance that was slightly ruined by the addition of a bell tower in the 19th century. Despite this anomaly, the building remains quite imposing with an exterior and interior intended to create fear and awe in the minds of visiting worshippers. ⓐ Impasse Borgendael 1 ⓣ 02 511 7836 ⓛ 10.00–17.45 Tues–Sun ⓝ Metro: Trône

CULTURE

BELvue

Examine the history of the Belgian royal family at this museum chronicling the life and times of the illustrious clan. Of particular interest is an extensive collection of items once owned and used by King Baudouin I. ⓐ Place des Palais 7 ⓣ 070 22 04 92 ⓦ www.belvue.be ⓛ 10.00–17.00 Tues–Fri, 10.00–18.00 Sat & Sun ⓝ Metro: Trône ⓘ Admission charge

Cinémathèque

Film buffs will love this museum, which looks at the dawn of film and early cinematography. It is still possible to catch a silent film in the working cinema, as well as seasons of modern films. ⓐ Palais des Beaux-Arts, Rue Baron Horta 9 ⓣ 02 551 1919 ⓦ www.cinematheque.be ⓛ Museum: 09.30–17.30 Tues–Sun; films: times vary ⓝ Metro: Gare Centrale ⓘ Admission charge

Musée des Instruments de Musique

Housed in a former department store, it took over a decade of restoration to create this museum dedicated to musical instruments. The collection boasts more than 6,000 items, of which 1,500 are on revolving display. As Belgium is the home of the creator of the saxophone, it should come as no surprise that there is an extensive section examining the development of the instrument, including a number of bizarre prototypes. **ⓐ** Rue Montagne de la Cour 2 **ⓣ** 02 545 0130 **ⓦ** www.mim.fgov.be **ⓛ** 09.30–17.00 Tues–Fri, 10.00–17.00 Sat & Sun **ⓝ** Metro: Gare Centrale

Musée Magritte

Housed in the Musées Royaux des Beaux-Arts (see below), this new museum, dedicated to the Belgian surrealist René Magritte (1898–1967), shows more than 200 of his works spanning his whole career, including drawings, sculptures and advertising posters. Use the entrance on Place Royale if you have pre-booked tickets, otherwise enter via the main museum entrance. **ⓐ** Rue de la Régence 3 **ⓣ** 02 508 3211 **ⓦ** www.musee-magritte-museum.be **ⓛ** 10.00–17.00 Tues & Thur–Sun, 10.00–20.00 Wed **ⓝ** Metro: Porte de Namur/Louise

Musées Royaux des Beaux-Arts

The Musées Royaux des Beaux-Arts (Royal Fine Arts Museum) is one of the finest in Belgium. The main collection is divided into two branches, each devoted to different periods: Ancient and Modern. A single admission fee will get you into both. However, you may want to break it up a bit as the place is vast.

The collection is particularly strong on painters and artists originating from the Low Countries. The building also houses the Magritte Museum. Rue de la Régence 3 02 508 3232 www.fine-arts-museum.be 10.00–17.00 daily Admission charge Metro: Gare Centrale

Musée d'Art Ancien Flemish painters of the 15th century – the so-called 'Flemish Primitives' – revolutionised the art world with their innovative use of oils. This extensive museum holds many of the finest works from the period, including paintings by Hieronymus Bosch, Rogier vander Weyden and Hans Memling. Go up a floor for the true masterpieces. Here is where you will find stunning works by favourite sons Rubens, Van Dyck, Jordaans, Breughel the Younger and, particularly, Breughel the Elder. For more modern work, go to the Musée d'Art Moderne just next door.

Musée d'Art Moderne The collection showcases works dating from the turn of the 20th century to the present day with a strong focus on Expressionism and Surrealism. Paul Delvaux is well represented. English-language brochures and tours are available.

RETAIL THERAPY

Place du Grand Sablon The shopping and supping locale choice for the city's elite. A couple of hours spent patrolling through the boutiques and cafés that line the square and surrounding streets is sure to dent your wallet. During weekend mornings the upper end of the square is transformed into an antiques market. Definitely not for those on a budget. ⓐ Place du Grand Sablon Ⓝ Trams: 92, 93, 94

TAKING A BREAK

Le Cap Sablon £–££ ❶ Rest your weary feet at this comfortable brasserie with typical Belgian dishes livened up with unexpected spices. There is a terrace that is popular during the summer months, but you'll need to book a table and specify the section when making your reservation. ⓐ Rue Lebeau 75 ❶ 02 512 0170 ❶ 12.00–23.30 Mon–Wed, 12.00–24.00 Thur–Sun Ⓝ Metro: Gare Centrale

AFTER DARK

RESTAURANTS

Les Brigittines 'Aux Marchés de la Chapelle' £–££ ❷ For something simple and filling, head over to this Belgian eatery strong on brasserie-style dishes such as sauerkraut and dumplings. Not for those on a diet or vegetarians.
ⓐ Place de la Chapelle 5 ❶ 02 512 6891 ❶ 12.00–14.30, 19.00–22.30 Mon–Fri, 19.00–23.00 Sat

Lola ££ ❸ A popular and reliable restaurant serving high-quality Belgian food, including simple dishes such as roast chicken, in a modern setting. ⓐ Place du Grand Sablon 33 ❶ 02 514 2460 Ⓦ www.restolola.be ❶ 12.00–15.00, 18.30–23.00 Mon–Fri, 12.00–23.30 Sat & Sun Ⓝ Trams: 92, 93, 94

Le Poulbot de Bruxelles ££ ④ This French restaurant caters for the political crowds that come for the tasty, well-prepared dishes and informal atmosphere. Luckily, the fact that the bulk of the clientele work at the parliament buildings doesn't take anything away from the relaxed dining and presentation. ⓐ Rue de la Croix de Fer 29 ⓣ 02 513 3861 ⓛ 12.00–14.00, 19.00–22.00 Mon, Wed–Fri, 12.00–14.00 Tues, 19.00–22.00 Sat ⓝ Metro: Parc

La Clef des Champs ££–£££ ⑤ Provençal speciality restaurant that looks like it belongs on a street in France. Expect typical dishes from the region. ⓐ Rue de Rollebeek 23 ⓣ 02 512 1193 ⓦ www.clefdeschamps.be ⓛ 12.00–14.00, 19.30–22.00 Tues–Sun ⓝ Trams: 92, 93, 94

Maison du Boeuf £££ ⑥ There's plenty to choose from at this ritzy restaurant, but it's the beef that you should make a beeline for. The house speciality is rib steak roasted in salt – and you should order it if you have the appetite. Gentlemen should note that a jacket and tie are required. ⓐ Hilton Hotel, Boulevard de Waterloo 38 ⓣ 02 504 1334 ⓛ 12.00–14.30, 19.00–22.30 daily ⓝ Metro: Louise

BARS & NIGHTCLUBS
Le Bier Circus It isn't much to look at, but this bar is packed full of beer varieties. You might be a bit overwhelmed by the 17-page menu, but the knowledgeable bar staff will help you make an informed selection. ⓐ Rue de l'Enseignement 57 ⓣ 02 218 0034 ⓦ www.bier-circus.be ⓛ 12.00–14.30, 18.00–23.00 Mon–Fri, 18.00–23.00 Sat ⓝ Trams: 92, 93, 94

Le Grain de Sable Customers flock to this cocktail-chic establishment due to its jazzy vibe that beckons and large, attractive streetside terrace. The clientele tends to be of the new money, upmarket brigade – but it's a nice place to enjoy a drink nonetheless. ⓐ Place du Grand Sablon 15 ① 02 514 0583 ① 08.00–late daily ⓝ Trams: 92, 93, 94

Le Perroquet In summer months this jewel of an Art Nouveau establishment is packed with the young, rich and fabulous of the city. However, as the grey months roll in so do the Eurocrats – and the atmosphere turns a tad dour. Go before the after-work rush if you want to bag a seat. ⓐ Rue Watteeu 31 ① 02 512 9922 ① 10.00–01.00 daily ⓝ Trams: 92, 93, 94

CINEMAS & THEATRES

Théâtre du Rideau de Bruxelles This French-language theatre company is a good place to go if you're looking for safe, reliable productions of historical dramas and modern classics. ⓐ Palais des Beaux-Arts, Rue Ravenstein 23 ① 02 507 8361 ⓦ www.rideaudebruxelles.be ① Box office: 11.00–19.00 Mon–Sat ⓝ Metro: Gare Centrale

Théâtre Royal du Parc This playhouse, built in 1782, is a real gem. While the productions aren't necessarily at the forefront of theatrical innovation, the interiors should be more than enough to convince you to buy a ticket. ⓐ Rue de la Loi 3 ① 02 505 3030 ⓦ www.theatreduparc.be ① Box office: 11.00–18.00 Mon–Fri, 11.00–13.00, 14.00–18.00 Sat & Sun ⓝ Metro: Arts-Loi or Parc

Beyond the petite ceinture

The neighbourhoods outside the petite ceinture (the ring of
boulevards surrounding the Upper and Lower Town) differ
greatly in flavour and form. The EU district is tailor-made for
government Eurocrats, while Ixelles is packed with colour
and excitement due to a vibrant African community. Visitors
should be sure to venture beyond the petite ceinture circle.

SIGHTS & ATTRACTIONS

Atomium

This symbol of the city was built as part of the World's Fair
celebrations of 1958. It reopened in 2006 after a renovation that
completely transformed the once tired exhibits, and the
structure is again a sight worth seeing. The trip to the top is a

● *View Brussels from the windows of the Atomium*

'must do' Brussels experience for most visitors and is well worth the admission charge. Boulevard du Centenaire 02 475 4777 www.atomium.be 10.00–18.00 daily. Box office closes 17.30 Metro: Heysel Admission charge

Bois de la Cambre

This vast park is the largest green space in the city. Located on the edge of the city centre, it was originally a section of a much larger forest that was reshaped to allow an avenue to be built through it for access to the countryside. Trams: 92, 93, 94

Collégiale des Saints Pierre et Guidon

The site of this church is one of the oldest in the city, dating back to the 10th century. The current structure was built in the 15th century in the Gothic style and is known for its Romanesque crypts. Place de la Valliance 02 527 9197 09.00–12.00, 14.00–17.00 daily Metro: St-Guidon

Ixelles

At its peak, Belgium had large interests in the Congo and equatorial Africa. While the country's legacy as a colonial nation is murky, Brussels benefited from an influx of citizens from the region. Ixelles is the neighbourhood where most reside in a colourful conglomeration of markets, restaurants and ethnic shops. Asian and North Africans also call the area home, making this the district to head to if you want a break from Dutch and French. The neighbourhood's centre is located at the corner of Rue Longue Vie and Rue de la Paix

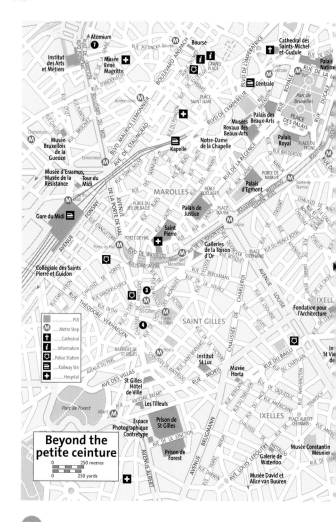

Beyond the
petite ceinture

0 ———— 250 metres
0 ———— 250 yards

POI
Ⓜ Metro Stop
✝ Cathedral
ⓘ Information
🅿 Police Station
🚆 Railway Stn
✚ Hospital

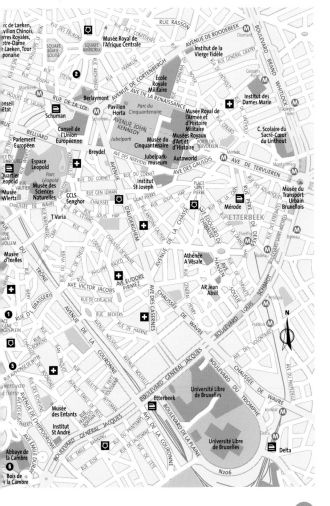

PARC DU CINQUANTENAIRE

This massive park is one of the green lungs of the city and home to some of its finest museums. King Léopold II shipped in more than 300 labourers to work around the clock to create the neoclassical building housing the park's various museums. The most famous structure inside the park is the Arc de Triomphe, a celebratory arch set for completion in 1880 to commemorate the 50th anniversary of the founding of the Belgian nation. Unfortunately, the deadline was missed by about 30 years. Also of note is the Pavillon Horta in the northwest section of the park, which holds a collection of reliefs by the artist Jef Lambeaux.

ⓐ Parq du Cinquantenaire Ⓜ Metro: Schuman

Notre-Dame de Laeken

This massive church just across the Avenue de la Reine from the Park de Laeken is a salute to the Gothic style and was completed in the mid-19th century. The cemetery holds tombs of important locals and a cast of Rodin's *The Thinker*. ⓐ Parvis Notre Dame ☎ 02 478 2095 🕓 14.00–17.00 Tues–Sun Ⓜ Metro: Bockstael

Pavillon Chinois

This pavilion was originally built as a restaurant for the royal family and now holds a collection of fine Chinese porcelain. ⓐ Rue Jules van Praet 44 ☎ 02 268 1608 🌐 www.kmkg-mrah.be 🕓 09.30–17.00 Tues–Fri, 10.00–17.00 Sat & Sun Ⓜ Trams: 23, 52 ❶ Admission charge

Serres Royales

Eleven linked greenhouses were commissioned by Léopold II and designed by a young Horta in the 1870s. A favourite with the royal family, many members have set up offices and audience areas within the leafy confines. Normally closed to the public, the greenhouses open to the hoi polloi every year in the month of May. ⓐ Avenue du Parc Royal 61 ⓣ 02 551 2020 ⓛ hours vary each May; check in advance with tourist office for schedules ⓝ Metro: Heysel ⓘ Admission charge

Tour Japonaise

Temporary Japanese exhibitions are held in the faux pagoda surrounded by elegant Japanese gardens. ⓐ Avenue Jules van Praet 44 ⓣ 02 268 1608 ⓦ www.kmkg-mrah.be ⓛ 09.30–17.00 Tues–Fri, 10.00–17.00 Sat & Sun ⓝ Trams: 23, 52 ⓘ Admission charge

▲ You'll find more art collections at the Pavillon Horta

CULTURE

Autoworld

This comprehensive auto museum chronicles the history of the automobile from 1886 to today. ⓐ Parc du Cinquantenaire 11 ⓣ 02 736 4165 ⓦ www.autoworld.be ⓛ 10.00–18.00 daily (Apr–Oct); 10.00–17.00 daily (Nov–Mar) ⓜ Metro: Mérode ⓘ Admission charge

Espace Photographique Contretype

This gallery houses a collection of photography and sponsors artist-in-residence programmes with regular showcases of their work. ⓐ Avenue de la Jonction 1 ⓣ 02 538 4220 ⓦ www.contretype.org ⓛ 11.00–18.00 Wed–Fri, 13.00–18.00 Sat & Sun ⓜ Trams: 81, 90, 92; Bus: 54 ⓘ Admission charge

Fondation pour l'Architecture

Tells the story of Brussels' architectural treasures. ⓐ Rue de l'Ermitage 55 ⓣ 02 642 2480 ⓦ www.fondationpourlarchitecture.be ⓛ 12.00–18.00 Tues & Thur–Sun, 12.00–19.00 Wed ⓜ Trams: 81, 82, 93, 94; Buses: 38, 54, 60 ⓘ Admission charge

Musée des Sciences Naturelles

Belgium's Royal Natural History Museum boasts a great collection of iguanodons and a stunning new room dedicated to evolution and the Arctic and Antarctic environments. ⓐ Rue Vautier 29 ⓣ 02 627 4238 ⓦ www.sciencesnaturelles.be ⓛ 09.30–16.45 Tues–Fri, 10.00–18.00 Sat & Sun ⓜ Metro: Trône/Maelbeck ⓘ Admission charge

◆ *Espace Photographique Contretype houses photographic art*

Musée Bruxellois de la Gueuze

This museum is made for beer fans as it takes visitors on a tasting tour around the final brewery that produces Gueuze – an intriguing beer that undergoes a fermenting process unique to the area. Rue Gheude 56 02 521 4928 www.cantillon.be 09.00–17.00 Mon–Fri, 10.00–17.00 Sat Metro: Clemenceau

Musée d'Ixelles

This enjoyable museum has a choice selection of modern art from the likes of Magritte, Delveaux and Toulouse-Lautrec. The exhibition spaces are small but perfectly formed. Rue Van Volsem 71 02 515 6421 11.30–17.00 Tues–Sun Buses: 38, 54, 60, 71 Admission charge

Musée David et Alice van Buuren

Art Deco is celebrated at this home of the wealthy collectors addicted to the movement. The clean lines of the architecture act as a beautiful backdrop to the art collection, which includes works by Brueghel and Van Gogh. Avenue Léo Errera 41 02 343 4851 www.museumvanbuuren.com 14.00–17.30 Wed–Mon Trams: 23, 24; Buses: 38, 60 Admission charge

Musée d'Erasmus

The 16th-century Dutch humanist and theologist Erasmus stayed in this home whenever he was in town. Copies of some of his most famous works along with letters from the ruling royal family addressed to him are on display. Rue de Chapitre 31 02 521 1383 www.erasmushouse.museum 10.00–17.00 Tues–Sun Metro: St-Guidon Admission charge

Musée Horta

The noted Art Nouveau architect Victor Horta completed this home and studio in 1901. While the exterior is impressive, it's what's inside that counts. Every detail is flawless right down to the door handles. Visit on a weekday to avoid the crowds.
ⓐ Rue Américaine 25 ⓣ 02 543 0490 ⓦ www.hortamuseum.be
ⓛ 14.00–17.30 Tues–Sun ⓝ Trams: 81, 92, 97; Bus: 54
ⓘ Admission charge

Musée René Magritte

Magritte painted many of his works in the living room at the rear of this home. The museum now holds many of the artist's personal effects and letters. ⓐ Rue Esseghem 135 ⓣ 02 428 2626
ⓦ www.magrittemuseum.be ⓛ 10.00–18.00 Wed–Sun
ⓝ Metro: Bockstael ⓘ Admission charge. This is not the same as the Magritte Museum

Musée de la Résistance

The Belgian Resistance movement is honoured by this museum consisting of documents that chronicle its years of struggle.
ⓐ Rue Van Lint 14 ⓣ 02 522 4041 ⓛ 09.00–12.00, 13.00–16.00
Mon, Tues, Thur & Fri ⓝ Metro: Clemenceau

Musée Royal de l'Afrique Centrale

This museum dedicated to the history and culture of Belgium's former African colonies is finally being dragged into the modern age with a major renovation of all the rooms currently under way with completion set for some time in 2011. Displays include archival notes taken from the files of the explorer Henry

Stanley and a famous crocodile gallery that remains in the same form as its original 1910 set-up. ⓐ Chaussée de Louvain 13 ⓣ 02 769 5211 ⓦ www.africamuseum.be ⓛ 10.00–17.00 Tues–Fri, 10.00–18.00 Sat & Sun ⓝ Tram: 44 ⓘ Admission charge

Musée Royal de l'Armée et d'Histoire Militaire

You'd expect a museum dedicated to the military to be pretty good in a country that has been fought over so many times – and you'd be right. The room featuring aircraft from the two world wars is particularly interesting. ⓐ Parc du Cinquantenaire 3 ⓣ 02 737 7811 ⓦ www.klm-mra.be ⓛ 09.00–12.00, 13.00–16.45 Tues–Sun ⓝ Metro: Mérode

Musées Royaux d'Art et d'Histoire

This large museum boasts a vast collection of antiquities from various historic global empires. While there aren't any real standout items, the sheer number of pieces is enough to warrant a visit. ⓐ Parc du Cinquantenaire 10 ⓣ 02 741 7211 ⓦ www.kmkg-mrah.be ⓛ 09.30–17.00 Tues–Fri, 10.00–17.00 Sat & Sun ⓦ Metro: Mérode

Musée du Transport Urbain Bruxellois

Visit this museum for a glimpse of the various methods of transport that once helped Brussels' residents travel across the city. The restored trams and buses date back to 1869. Alternatively, take a ride on one yourself by boarding the old-fashioned tram that travels between the Parc du Cinquantenaire and Tervueren. ⓐ Avenue de Tervueren 364

❶ 02 515 3108 Ⓦ www.trammuseumbrussels.be ❸ 13.30–18.30 Sat & Sun (Apr–Oct) Ⓝ Tram: 39, 44 ❶ Admission charge

Musée Wiertz

Back in his day (1805–65), Antoine Wiertz was a legend in his own mind. Famous for painting massive biblical and mythical scenes, he convinced the Belgian government to purchase him a house and studio in return for inheriting his works after his death. This museum is the end result. ⓐ Rue Vautier 62 ❶ 02 648 1718 Ⓦ www.fine-arts-museum.be ❸ 10.00–12.00, 13.00–17.00 Tues–Fri & every 2nd Sat & Sun Ⓝ Metro: Trône

RETAIL THERAPY

Outside of the petite ceinture, you'll find the ultimate in luxury and fresh and funky street markets. For the big designer names, look to Avenue Louise and the Boulevard de Waterloo where you'll find Chanel, Gucci and Bulgari (among others). Mid-range labels can be found on the Avenue de la Toison d'Or where high-street names are in abundance dotted throughout the galleries that run off the main street. For ethnic finds and foods, look on the Chaussée de Wavre, which runs from Porte de Namur. Meanwhile, bohemian and unique boutiques can be found on Rue St Boniface. Finally, Rue du Bailli is the place to go for shoes, chain stores and chic cafés.

TAKING A BREAK

Café Belga £ ❶ An outdoor patio and sleek looks draw a crowd of artsy and wealthy media types. While it's more expensive than average, the interiors will make you feel like you're part of the cool club. ⓐ Place Eugene Flagey-Plein 18 ⓣ 02 640 3508 ⓦ www.cafebelga.be ⓛ 09.30–14.00 Mon–Thur & Sun, 09.30–03.00 Fri & Sat ⓝ Bus: 71

Kafeneio £ ❷ Crowds flock to this buffet meze bar with more than 50 hot and cold Mediterranean dishes to choose from. ⓐ Rue Stevin 134 ⓣ 02 231 5555 ⓛ 12.00–23.00 ⓝ Metro: Schuman

AFTER DARK

RESTAURANTS

Mille et Une Nuits £–££ ❸ Camp and kitsch don't even begin to describe this Tunisian restaurant designed to look like a Bedouin tent. Surprisingly, the food is mouthwateringly good with service to match. ⓐ Rue de Moscou 7 ⓣ 02 537 4127 ⓦ www.milleetunenuits.be ⓛ 12.00–15.00, 18.00–23.30 Mon–Sat ⓝ Metro: Parvis de St-Gilles

L'Elément Terre ££ ❹ This venerable vegetarian establishment is one of the best in town. It features intriguing combinations and the finest in fresh organic ingredients. If you're willing to dabble, go for the discovery plate and have a little taste of everything. ⓐ Chaussée de Waterloo 465 ⓣ 02 649 3727 ⓛ 12.00–14.30, 19.00–22.30 Tues–Fri, 19.00–22.30 Sat ⓝ Trams: 91, 92

Chez Marie ££–£££ ❺ Once a neighbourhood establishment, this French restaurant is now one of the hardest to get a

table at – and all due to a single Michelin star. Interiors are cosy, with fresh ingredients ensuring that everything is packed with flavour without getting too heavy.
ⓐ Rue Alphonse de Witte 40 ⓣ 02 644 3031 ⓛ 12.00–14.15, 19.30–22.30 Tues–Fri, 19.30–22.30 Sat Ⓝ Trams: 81, 82; Bus: 71

La Porte des Indes £££ ⓿ If you thought the UK had a lock on great Indian restaurants, then you'd be mistaken. This classy establishment takes the cuisine to another level and features dishes you won't find at your local takeaway. Southern Indian cuisine is the speciality, but you'll have to spend a lot for the privilege.
ⓐ Avenue Louise 455 ⓣ 02 647 8651 ⓦ www.laportedesindes.com
ⓛ 12.00–14.30, 19.00–22.30 Mon–Thur, 12.00–14.30, 19.00–23.00 Fri & Sat, 19.00–22.30 Sun Ⓝ Trams: 93, 94

Restaurant Bruneau £££ ⓿ Restaurant Bruneau has two Michelin stars, and is an essential stop for fans of food. While it's far from the city centre, it's worth the trek. However, you might need a mortgage to afford the menu, which features dishes that cost anything from €40–100 per course. ⓐ Avenue Broustin 75
ⓣ 02 421 7070 ⓦ www.bruneau.be ⓛ 12.00–14.00, 19.00–22.00 Mon, Thur–Sun Ⓝ Metro: Simonis

BARS & NIGHTCLUBS

Fat Boys Mix with the expats at this popular sports bar hangout. So if you're missing the Premiership scores, or Ashes recaps, you know where to go. ⓐ Place du Luxembourg 5 ⓣ 02 511 3266
ⓦ www.fatboys-be.com ⓛ daily 11.00–late Ⓝ Metro: Trône

L'Horloge du Sud Caribbean rums, live African music, R&B dance nights – it's all here at this great bar in the heart of the Ixelles African community. You can even nibble on fantastic African/Belgian fusion cuisine. ⓐ Rue du Trône 141 ⓣ 02 512 1864 ⓦ www.horlogedusud.be ⓛ 11.00–01.00 Mon–Fri, 17.00–01.00 Sat & Sun ⓝ Metro: Trône

CINEMAS & THEATRES

Théâtre 140 Physical theatre is the speciality of this innovative company under the direction of Jo Dekmine – a man who has been on the local scene for decades and has worked with many artists of high calibre, including Jacques Brel, Serge Gainsbourg and Pink Floyd. ⓐ Avenue Eugéne Plasky 140 ⓣ 02 733 9708 ⓦ www.theatre140.be ⓛ Box office: 12.00–18.00 Mon–Fri ⓝ Metro: Diamant

Théâtre de la Toison d'Or Wild and crazy revue-style comedy is what to expect at this venue specialising in satire. ⓐ Galeries de la Toison d'Or 396 ⓣ 02 510 0510 ⓦ www.theatredelatoisondor.be ⓛ Box office: 10.00–16.00 Mon, 10.00–18.00 Tues–Fri, 14.00–18.00 Sat ⓝ Metro: Porte de Namur

---

● *Book a tour of the Stella Artois building in Leuven*

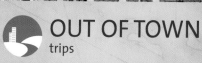

OUT OF TOWN
trips

Antwerp

For great designer shopping, a peek inside the high-stakes world of the diamond industry, stunning art collections, capital clubbing and hip neighbourhoods in the form of the transformed waterfront warehouse district of Het Eilandje, Antwerp can't be beaten. Go for a day or spend an even longer period in this city that Rubens once called home.

GETTING THERE

Four trains an hour make the journey between Antwerp and Brussels, taking 40 minutes to reach their destination. Alternatively, it's a quick 30- to 45-minute drive along the A12 or E19/A1 motorways.

SIGHTS & ATTRACTIONS

Grote Markt

Brussels may boast the Grand Place, but Antwerp rivals the capital city in terms of stunning squares in the form of the Grote Markt. The spiritual heart of the city, the square offers up the most important architecture and historical buildings in Antwerp.
ⓐ Grote Markt

Onze-Lieve-Vrouwekathedraal

This church is the largest Gothic church in the Low Countries and continues to dominate Antwerp's skyline. Despite the beauty of the interiors, it is the artwork that draws the crowds,

🔺 Antwerp's Grote Markt rivals Brussels' Grand Place

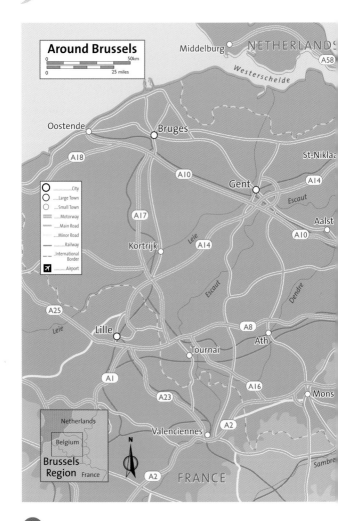

including four large works by Rubens and significant works by de Backer and others. ⓐ Groenplaats 21 ⓣ 03 213 9951 ⓦ www.dekathedraal.be ⓛ 10.00–17.00 Mon–Fri, 10.00–15.00 Sat, 13.00–16.00 Sun ⓘ Admission charge

Rubenshuis

Antwerp's favourite son, the painter Rubens, bought this house in 1610 and used it as his studio until the day of his death. Step inside for a peek into what 17th-century Belgian life was like. ⓐ Wapper 9–11 ⓣ 03 201 1555 ⓛ 10.00–17.00 Tues–Sun ⓘ Admission charge

Sint Carolus Borromeuskerk

At the height of the Counter-Reformation, the Jesuits built this church to honour the leader of the movement, the Archbishop of Milan. The interior décor squad wasn't bad. Rubens and his students completed 39 ceiling paintings to decorate the interior. Unfortunately, a fire destroyed them all in 1718. Despite this incident, the church's beauty remained and the façade is still a highlight in this city of spectacular architecture. ⓐ Hendrik Conscienceplein 6 ⓣ 03 272 2 023 ⓛ 10.00–12.30, 14.00–17.00 Mon–Sat

Sint-Pauluskerk

This church boasts the richest art collection in Antwerp. While its original Gothic architecture has been somewhat obscured by more recent Baroque additions, the interior remains inspiring. Highlights include works by Rubens and Van Dyck. ⓐ Nosestraat ⓣ 03 232 3267 ⓛ daily 14.00–17.00 (May–Sept)

Stadhuis

Considered by many to be a symbol of the city, the Stadhuis is actually Antwerp's celebrated town hall built in the Flemish–Italian Renaissance style. Both the exterior and the interior are impressive. ⓐ Grote Markt ⓣ 03 220 8020 ⓦ www.antwerpen.be ⓛ Tours: 14.00 Mon–Thur ⓘ Admission charge

Vlaeykensang

Go through the gate at No 16 Oude Koornmarkt to find this maze of alleys dating back to the 16th century, and you'll experience a quiet contemplation away from the hordes.

CULTURE

Klank van de Stad

Formerly the city's meat market, this museum is the latest addition to Antwerp's cultural scene. Occasional concerts and vast collections of music and musical instruments chronicle the history and development of 'City Sounds'. ⓐ Vleeshouwersstraat 38–40 ⓣ 03 233 6100 ⓛ 10.00–17.00 Tues–Sun ⓘ Admission charge

Koninklijk Museum voor Schone Kunsten (KMSK) Antwerpen (Royal Museum of Fine Arts)

One of the most important collections in Europe with around 7,000 works. Highlights include paintings by Van Eyck, Breughel the Younger, Magritte and Rubens. The museum closed at the end of 2010 and will reopen in 2012. Its core collection will move to MAS during the renovation (see page 109). ⓐ Leopold de

Waelplaats 2 ☏ 03 238 7809 ⓦ www.kmska.be ⓛ 10.00–17.00 Tues–Sat, 10.00–18.00 Sun ⓘ Admission charge

Mayer van den Bergh Museum
A wealthy merchant compiled this collection of art treasures from the Low Countries. Masterpieces include works by Breughel the Elder, along with priceless tapestries, sculptures

⬥ *MoMu – Antwerp's innovative fashion museum*

and examples of stained glass. ⓐ Lange Gasthuisstraat 19
ⓣ 03 232 4237 ⓦ http://museum.antwerpen.be ⓛ 10.00–17.00
Tues–Sun ⓘ Admission charge

MoMu (Mode Museum)

This museum is dedicated to fashion and is probably the
most dynamic museum in Antwerp. The permanent collection
chronicling the history of fashion is remarkable, but it is
the innovative temporary exhibits that draw the masses.
ⓐ Nationalestraat 28 ⓣ 03 470 2770 ⓦ www.momu.be
ⓛ 10.00–18.00 Tues–Sun, 10.00–21.00 1st Thur of month
ⓘ Admission charge

Museum Aan de Stroom (MAS)

This new museum, housed in a tower 60m (197ft) high, is part
of the redevelopment of the Eilandje area, where Antwerp's
oldest docks are. Due to open fully in May 2011, it will house
both temporary and permanent exhibitions celebrating
Antwerp's history as a port. The Nationaal Scheepvaartmuseum
(National Maritime Museum), with models of boats and
exhibits on the development of shipping, is due to move here, as
is the core collection of the fine art museum (KMSK) until its
renovation is completed in 2012. The city's ethnographic
museum will also move here. MAS has an attractive café on the
ground floor, and you can get a panoramic view of the river and
port from higher up. ⓐ Hanzestedenplaats 1 ⓣ 03 206 0940
ⓛ Opening times are likely to be similar to Antwerp's other
leading museums. Check ⓦ www.mas.be for further details
ⓘ Admission charge

Museum van Hedendaagse Kunst Antwerpen (MuHKA)

Once a grain silo, the MuHKA (Museum of Contemporary Art)
exhibits art from the 1970s onwards. This brief places it at
the cutting edge of the art world and its reputation among
those in the know is extremely high. The permanent collection
of 700 works is rarely displayed in favour of radical temporary
exhibitions. Both Belgian and international artists are
supported and represented. Those with children should head
straight to the first floor 'MUST for Kids' section, which is
packed with toys and games inspired by art. ⓐ Leuvenstraat 32
ⓘ 03 206 9999 ⓦ www.muhka.be ⓛ 11.00–18.00 Tues–Sun
ⓘ Admission charge

Plantin-Moretus Museum

This museum chronicling Flemish printing practices from
the 15th to the 18th century is actually a real find. Many printers
during this period worked at home in order to create works
for their private library – so not only do you get a lesson in
bookmaking, but you also get to learn more about the elite
lifestyles of the period. ⓐ Vrijdagmarkt 22–23 ⓘ 03 221 1450
ⓦ http://museum.antwerpen.be ⓛ 10.00–17.00 Tues–Sun
ⓘ Admission charge

Provinciaal Diamantmuseum

Three floors of the rock that's a girl's best friend. This interactive
museum chronicles the journey of diamonds from rough stone
to polished treasure. ⓐ Koningin Astridplein 19–23 ⓘ 03 202 4890
ⓦ www.diamantmuseum.be ⓛ 10.00–17.30 Thur–Tues (Feb–Dec)
ⓘ Admission charge

RETAIL THERAPY

Antwerp has been known as a high fashion destination ever since the famous Antwerp Six designers dominated London Fashion Week in the late 1980s. Today, names like Dries Van Noten, Ann Demeulemeester, Martin Margiela, Raf Simons, Dirk Bikkembergs and Wim Neels are splashed across the pages of fashion magazines on a regular basis.

Pick up a few designer pieces by wandering the streets of Antwerp's two hippest neighbourhoods: Het Eilandje and Het Zuid. Alternatively, do as the locals do and shop 'The Meir' at weekends when this becomes *the* place to see and be seen.

TAKING A BREAK

Grand Café Horta £ This café, located in the Art Nouveau masterpiece Horta Complex, is a great place to try some Belgian specialities. The perfect spot to combine both visual and taste sensations while exploring the neighbourhood. ⓐ Hopland 2 ❶ 03 232 2815 ⓦ www.grandcafehorta.be ⓛ 09.00–23.00 Mon–Fri, 09.00–24.00 Sat & Sun. Food from 11.00

AFTER DARK

RESTAURANTS
Den Rooden Hoed £–££ Dating from 1750, this restaurant is the oldest in Antwerp. The cuisine is solid, the service welcoming.

The 16th-century wine cellar is a wine connoisseur's dream.
ⓐ Oude Koornmarkt 25 ⓣ 03 233 2844 ⓛ 12.00–14.00, 18.00–22.30
Mon–Thur, till 23.00 Fri & Sat, till 22.00 Sun

De Broers van Julienne ££ Vegetarians will love this meat-free
restaurant with a Middle-Eastern twist. ⓐ Kasteelpleinstraat
45–47 ⓣ 03 232 0203 ⓦ www.debroersvanjulienne.be
ⓛ 12.00–22.30 Mon–Sat, 18.00–22.30 Sun

The Glorious ££ This stylish and atmospheric new bistro and
wine bar with a creative menu is often packed. It is conveniently
located near both the Fine Art and Contemporary Art museums.
ⓐ De Burburestraat 4a ⓣ 03 237 0613 ⓦ www.theglorious.be
ⓛ 10.00–01.00 Tues–Sat, 12.00–23.00 Sun

Het Pomphuis £££ For a true blow-out meal, go straight
to this converted Art Nouveau pumping station. You'll
need to take a taxi to get there but the waterside views make
up for the inconvenience. Although it resembles a French
brasserie, the cuisine is actually Pacific Rim inspired.
ⓐ Siberiastraat z/n ⓣ 03 770 8625 ⓦ www.hetpomphuis.be
ⓛ 12.00–15.00, 18.00–22.30 Mon–Thur, till 23.00 Fri &
Sat, 12.00–22.00 Sun

Huis de Colvenier £££ This landmark establishment is truly
one of the top spots in town in which to bag a table. Seriously
fine French cuisine is what's on offer in the romantic salons.
ⓐ Sint-Antoniusstraat 8 ⓣ 03 226 6573 ⓦ www.colvenier.be
ⓛ 12.00–15.00, 18.30–22.00 Tues–Fri, 18.30–22.00 Sat

BARS & NIGHTCLUBS

Café D'Anvers First it was a church. Then it was a cinema. Today, it's a deep house club. Around since 1991, it's a solid favourite with locals looking for uplifting beats. ⓐ Verversrui 15 ⓣ 03 226 3870 ⓦ www.cafe-d-anvers.com ⓛ 23.00–07.00 Fri & Sat

Den Engel Antwerp's oldest bar, this institution on Grote Markt only closes once the last customer leaves, so it can be open days on end considering the support of its character-filled regular clientele. A great place for a pre-club tipple or a post-big-night wind-down. ⓐ Grote Markt 3 ⓣ 03 233 1252 ⓛ daily 09.00–late

Red & Blue The most debauched club in Belgium. Fridays are mixed, Saturdays as gay as gay can be. Grace Jones once famously drove a stretch limo through the crowd of clubbers on the dance floor. ⓐ Lange Schipperkapelstraat 11–13 ⓣ 03 213 0555 ⓦ wwwredandblue.be ⓛ 23.00–late Fri, 23.00–07.00 Sat

SIPS Opened in 2000, SIPS has established itself as probably the best cocktail bar in Antwerp, run by a former head barman on the QE2. He uses classic cocktail recipes, as well as creating his own. ⓐ Gillisplaats 8 ⓣ 0477 639152 ⓦ www.sips-cocktails.com ⓛ 17.00–late Mon–Thur, 18.00–late Fri & Sat

Velvet Lounge Modelled on the Buddha Bar in Paris, this late-night chill-out spot is ultra-hip and usually packed. Patrons are often dressed to the nines. ⓐ Luikstraat 6 ⓣ 03 237 3978 ⓦ www.velvetlounge.be ⓛ 17.30–late Mon–Fri, 18.00–late Sat & Sun

CINEMAS & THEATRES

Bourlaschouwburg The Bourla theatre was built in the 1830s as a centre for theatre and opera. Renovation was completed in 1993 when Antwerp became the European Capital of Culture. ⓐ Komedieplaats 18 ☎ 03 231 0750

Cartoon's Situated directly opposite the Steen, Cartoon's hosts the best of alternative cinema. The coffee isn't bad either. ⓐ Kaasstraat 4–6 ☎ 03 232 9632 ⓦ www.cartoons-cinema.be

Sint-Augustinuskerk This deconsecrated church now offers a packed schedule of concerts, cultural events and exhibitions. ⓐ Kammenstraat 73 ☎ 03 229 1880

ACCOMMODATION

T'Elzenveld ££ Housed in the medieval buildings of a former hospital, this hotel offers period furniture in a garden setting. ⓐ Lange Gasthuisstraat 45 ☎ 03 202 7770 ⓦ www.elzenveld.be

Park Inn ££ A new hotel near Centraal station, the zoo and the Diamond Museum, with comfortable rooms with free Internet access. There's no bar or room service, but you can hardly do better for the price and location. ⓐ Koningin Astridplein 14 ☎ 03 202 3170 ⓦ www.antwerpen.parkinn.be

Julien ££–£££ With 22 rooms, a bar and a spa, the Julien is the epitome of contemporary style, decorated in white and pale colours. ⓐ Korte Nieuwstraat 24 ☎ 03 229 0600 ⓦ www.hotel-julien.com

Waterloo & Leuven

WATERLOO

The great battle at Waterloo changed the course of European history and destroyed the illustrious career of Napoleon. Thousands of visitors descend on the fields to the south of the town every year in order to witness the location that played a crucial role in the downfall of an emperor.

A visit invariably begins at the visitor centre. An audiovisual presentation of the tactics involved in the battle is included in the cost of admission and well worth watching if you want to get an idea of the scale of the fighting.

These days, the town of Waterloo may not be much to look at, acting as little more than a suburb of Brussels. However, things have improved in recent years, as the ongoing restoration of a collection of 19th-century buildings and the introduction of scale models and films has seen the destination become far more informative and upmarket.

The latest addition to the experience is a battlefield bus tour (with recorded commentary in English, French and Flemish), which will give you as good an overview of the battle and its geography as you can get. All the attractions on the site have now been brought together (with the same opening times) so that you only need one ticket, the Pass 1815, available from the tourist office in Waterloo (opposite the Wellington Museum) or from **Waterloo Visitor Centre** (ⓐ Route du Lion 315, Waterloo ❶ 02 385 1912 ⓦ www.waterloo1815.be ⓛ daily 09.30–18.30 (Apr–Oct); daily 10.00–17.00 (Nov–Mar) ❶ Admission charge).

GETTING THERE

From Brussels, it's a 50-minute journey by bus from Avenue Fonsny (near the Gare du Midi) to Waterloo. Buses run at half-hour intervals. Alternatively, take one of the frequent commuter train services from the Gare du Midi. Journey time is 15 minutes.

Five trains an hour depart Brussels for Leuven. The journey time is approximately 35 minutes. Alternatively, take the E40/A3 motorway east directly to the town.

SIGHTS & ATTRACTIONS

Butte du Lion

Erected by the Dutch ten years after the battle, this pyramid of 226 steps crowned by a lion provides stunning views over the famous battlefield.

Champ de Bataille

The Champ de Bataille is the actual battlefield on which the fighting was played out. Located south of the town of Waterloo, these rye fields were stained red with the blood of French, British and Prussian soldiers on 18 June 1815 when the British, under the leadership of the Duke of Wellington, were attacked by Napoleon's army. More than 48,000 people died during the course of the battle, especially in skirmishes around the fortified farms of La Sainte-Haye, Papelotte and Hougoumont. Every five years the Battle of Waterloo is re-enacted by uniformed participants from around the world. The event happens on the closest weekend to the battle's anniversary, with the next re-enactment scheduled for 2015.

⬥ *The lion memorial watches over the Champ de Bataille*

Panorama de la Bataille

Created in 1912, this circular painting of the charge of the French cavalry is actually quite breathtaking. The artist's use of perspective and realism seems to take you on to the battlefield. Listen closely and you might even hear the cannons.

CULTURE

Le Quartier Général de Napoléon (Napoleon's Last Headquarters, formerly the Musée du Caillou)

Packed with souvenirs and images of Napoleon, this museum located south of the battlefield in the town of Genappe contains the room where the formidable French emperor spent his last evening before the battle that resulted in his demise. Displayed in the room are some of his personal effects and a number of objects found on the field. ⓐ Chaussée de Bruxelles 66,

MUSÉE WELLINGTON

This former inn was the Duke of Wellington's headquarters during the fighting. Today, visitors will find displays that chronicle the events that occurred during the 100 days leading up to the Battle of Waterloo, plus maps and models of the battle itself. There are also a few items and souvenirs commemorating Wellington's victory.

ⓐ Chaussée de Bruxelles 147, Waterloo ⓣ 02 354 7806
ⓦ www.museewellington.be ⓛ 09.30–18.30 daily
(Apr–Oct); 10.00–17.00 daily (Nov–Mar) ⓘ Admission charge

Gemappe ☎ 02 384 2424 🕐 10.00–18.30 daily (Apr–Oct); 13.00–17.00 daily (Nov–Mar) ❶ Admission charge

TAKING A BREAK

Le Bivouac de l'Empereur £–££ Just opposite the visitor centre in an old inn. The food is surprisingly good, particularly the grills. Though tour parties end up there, locals also favour it. The décor is inspired by Napoleon. ⓐ Route du Lion ☎ 02 384 6740 ⓦ www.restaurantdulion.be 🕐 12.00–14.30, 18.30–22.30 Tues–Fri, 12.00–22.30 Sat & Sun

AFTER DARK

Restaurants

Brasserie du Couvent £–££ Cheerful and lively brasserie near the tourist office in Waterloo serving Belgian and French cuisine, and pasta dishes. ⓐ Rue du Couvent 7 ☎ 02 351 3834 ⓦ www.brasserieducouvent.be 🕐 Daily

L'Amusoir ££–£££ Filling yet well-prepared Belgian dishes and succulent *filet mignon* with a variety of sauces draw the numerous punters to this popular steakhouse in the centre of town. While the whitewashed building may look old and a little uncared for from the outside, the meals served up inside are sure to please. ⓐ Chaussée de Bruxelles 121 ☎ 02 354 8233 🕐 12.30–15.00, 18.00–22.30 daily

ACCOMMODATION

Hotel le Côté Vert ££ There aren't many quality places to stay in Waterloo. This comfortable, simple hotel, which also has

apartments and a restaurant, is one of the better ones. Expect cleanliness and a warm welcome. ❸ Chaussée de Bruxelles 200, Waterloo ❶ 02 354 0105 ❿ www.cotevert.be

LEUVEN

Which came first? The students or the beer? In this historic town no one is really sure, as this university centre has been known for both for centuries. This is Belgium's equivalent of Oxford, and is dotted with bicycles and picturesque lanes. This is also the home of Stella Artois, so for a drinking tour of the country, you couldn't choose a better location.

SIGHTS & ATTRACTIONS
Grote Markt
Leuven's main square, like most major Belgian cities, is its heart. Here is where you will find the treasures of the city's architecture, including the magnificent Stadhuis (town hall).

Sint-Pieterskerk
It may not be the prettiest church in Belgium, but Sint-Pieterskerk is fascinating for architecture fans due to the fact that it is essentially a failed project. Work on the church began in the early 15th century and continued for more than 100 years until locals decided to pull down some of the Romanesque towers in order to accommodate a new plan designed by the architect Joos Matsys. When it was discovered that the foundations were too weak, the project was abandoned and the end result is what you see today.

So if you think the exterior looks a little off, you wouldn't be mistaken. The towers were capped, creating an asymmetric look that is slightly at odds with what the eye is trained to appreciate. ⓐ Grote Markt ① 016 226 906 🕒 10.00–17.00 Mon–Fri, 10.00–16.30 Sat, 14.00–17.00 Sun (summer). Closed Mon in winter

Stadhuis

Leuven's Stadhuis (town hall) is a masterpiece of Gothic architecture complete with all the ornate flamboyance one would expect from the period. Completed in 1469, it has survived a lot during its 500-plus years of existence, including drastic fires and a bomb explosion at its doors in 1944 at the height of World War II. Tours are available in Flemish and English. ⓐ Grote Markt 9 ① 016 27 22 76 🕒 Tours: 11.00 & 15.00 Mon–Fri, 15.00 Sat & Sun (Apr–Sept); daily 15.00 (Oct–Mar)

● *Sint-Pieterskerk is interesting partly for its imperfections*

Stella Artois

Worship at the brewery that brought the world Stella Artois. A facility has been churning out beer on these grounds since 1366, but the drink we all know and love wasn't introduced until 1926. Reservations fill up fast so it is best to book well in advance. ⓐ Vaartkom 33 ⓣ 016 247 111 ⓛ Tours: by reservation only 09.00, 10.30, 13.00, 14.30, 16.00, 18.00 & 19.30 Tues–Sat; you can also reserve online at ⓦ www.breweryvisits.com ⓘ Admission charge

CULTURE

M

That's right: simply M – and a pleasant enough museum with a wealth of porcelain, plus collections of minor paintings and stained glass to highlight the fashions of the 16th century. ⓐ Vanderkelen Straat 28 ⓣ 016 27 29 29 ⓦ www.mleuven.be ⓛ 10.00–18.00 Tues–Sun ⓘ Admission charge

RETAIL THERAPY

Brusselsestraat market If it's Saturday and you're an early riser, then make a beeline for the farmers' market on Brusselsestraat. Pick up fresh produce, cheeses, meats and local delicacies while you enjoy the lively atmosphere. ⓛ 09.00–12.00 Sat

TAKING A BREAK

Ombre ou Soleil £ Mediterranean brasserie-style dining that's good for a light lunch or quiet meal away from the masses. Fish and meat specialities are served in a sun-filled space. ⓐ Muntstraat 20 ⓣ 016 225 187 ⓛ 12.00–15.00, 18.30–22.00 Mon–Fri, 18.30–22.00 Sat

AFTER DARK
Restaurants
Luzine ££–£££
Jeroen Meus's restaurant is one of the best in town, with excellent French and Belgian dishes, particularly fish. ⓐ Kolonel Begaultlaan 15 ⓣ 016 89 08 77 ⓦ www.restaurantluzine.be ⓛ daily 12.00–14.00, 19.00–21.00

Oesterbar £££ Many locals consider this place the best in town if you're hankering for fish or seafood. Unsurprisingly, oysters are the house speciality. In winter, an open log fire will warm your toes. ⓐ Muntstraat 23 ⓣ 016 290 600 ⓦ www.oesterbar.be ⓛ 12.00–14.30, 18.00–22.30 Mon, Tues & Fri, 18.00–22.30 Sat

De Troubadour £££ This restaurant is where the locals go when they're looking for something special. Noted for its grilled meats and fish. ⓐ Tiensestraat 32 ⓣ 016 225 065 ⓦ www.troubadour.be ⓛ 11.30–14.30, 17.30–22.30 Wed–Mon

Bars & Nightclubs
Domus More a café/bar than an actual club, this rustic drinking spot adjoins the Domus brewery and is famous for its honey beer. The kind of place to go to for a late evening of slow drinking with friends. ⓐ Tiensestraat 8 ⓣ 016 201 149 ⓦ www.domusleuven.be ⓛ 09.00–01.00 Tues–Thur & Sun, 09.00–02.00 Fri & Sat

Silo Club As a university town, Leuven has its fair share of clubs. Situated in a former warehouse, the Silo Club is one of Belgium's best. ⓐ Vaartkom 39 ⓣ 016 237 252 ⓦ www.silo.be ⓛ 23.00–late Thur–Sun

ACCOMMODATION

Daniels Bed & Breakfast **££** Small B&B with light, modern furnishings in a quiet residential quarter just west of the city centre. ⓐ Cardenberch 14 ⓣ 016 238 780 ⓦ www.danielsbedandbreakfast.be

Theater Hotel **££–£££** Contemporary 21-room property with an adjoining art gallery. The buffet breakfast is well worth waking up for. ⓐ Bondgenotenlaan 20 ⓣ 016 222 819 ⓦ www.theaterhotel.be

Martin's Kloosterhotel **£££** Splash out on this 16th-century town house with its modern rooms and luxurious amenities. ⓐ Predikherenstraat 22 ⓣ 016 213 141 ⓦ www.martins-hotels.com

---

ⓞ *Most train services to other parts of Belgium leave from Brussels Central*

PRACTICAL
information

Directory

GETTING THERE

By air

For a short stay, those coming from the UK can fly to Brussels from a number of regional airports. Brussels' Zaventem International Airport is located approximately 14 km (9 miles) northeast of the city centre. Those choosing to fly with Ryanair will land at Brussels South International Airport in Charleroi, situated 55 km (34 miles) away. The average flying time from London is one hour. See also page 48 for more details on airports.

Many people are aware that air travel emits CO_2, which contributes to climate change. You may be interested in the possibility of lessening the environmental impact of your flight through the charity **Climate Care** (ⓦ www.jpmorganclimatecare.com) which offsets your CO_2 by funding environmental projects around the world.

By rail

Travelling by rail is easy from the UK, and it provides the chance to see something of the countryside en route. The most common way is on Eurostar, which has ten departures a day (eight at weekends) between London's St Pancras International and Brussels. The total journey time is approximately two hours. If you intend to travel further in Belgium, it's best to book through Rail Europe.

The monthly *Thomas Cook European Rail Timetable* has up-to-date schedules for European international and domestic train services.

Eurostar reservations (UK) ☏ 08705 186 186 ⓦ www.eurostar.com
Rail Europe ☏ 0844 848 4070 ⓦ www.raileurope.co.uk
Thomas Cook Publishing ☏ (UK) 01733 416 477; (USA) 1 800 322 3834 ⓦ www.thomascookpublishing.com

By road

The Belgian motorway system is well integrated in the European motorway network. The easiest motorway to use is the E40/A10 if travelling from Ostend or the E40/A18, connecting with the E40/A10 if arriving by Eurotunnel into France. Driving in Belgium can be challenging as streets tend to be narrow and riddled with potholes once you leave the motorway. Congestion can sometimes be a problem, especially during traditional rush hours. One law to be aware of is the *priorité à droite* rule, which forces all cars to give way to any vehicle on the right – even on major roads. Trams always have right of way.

ⓘ Try to avoid arriving or departing during rush hours, which extend between 06.30–09.30 and 16.00–19.00.

ⓘ Belgian drivers are known to be aggressive, and the one-way street system is cause for confusion.

Long-distance buses connect Brussels with most other European countries. From London by Eurolines, the fastest direct journey time is about seven hours depending on connections.

Eurolines ⓦ www.eurolines.co.uk

ENTRY FORMALITIES

Visitors to Belgium who are citizens of the UK, Ireland, Australia, the USA, Canada or New Zealand will need a passport but not a visa for stays of up to three months. South African nationals do require a visa.

🅘 If you are travelling from other countries, you may need a visa; it is best to check before you leave home.

Customs

There are no customs controls at borders for visitors from EU countries. EU residents can bring in, or take out, goods without restrictions on quantity or value, as long as these goods are for personal use only. For visitors from outside the EU, most personal effects and the following items are duty free: one video camera or two still cameras with ten rolls of film each, a portable radio, a tape recorder and a laptop computer provided they show signs of use; 400 cigarettes or 50 cigars or 250 g of tobacco; 2 litres of wine or 1 litre of liquor per person over 17 years old; fishing gear; one bicycle; skis; tennis or squash racquets; and golf clubs.

🅘 As entry requirements and customs regulations are subject to change, you should always check the current situation with your local travel agent, airline, or a Belgian embassy or consulate before you leave.

MONEY

The currency in Belgium is the euro (€). A euro is divided into 100 cents. Coins are in denominations of 1, 2, 5, 10, 20 and 50 cents plus €1 and €2. Notes are available in denominations of €5, €10, €20 and €50. €100, €200 and €500 notes are also issued, but are rarely seen and not widely accepted due to the risk from counterfeiting. Try to bring cash in denominations no higher than €50 if you can. You can withdraw money using ATMs at many Belgian banks. The most widely accepted credit cards are Mastercard, American Express and Visa.

🛈 Many smaller businesses, including some restaurants, taverns, smaller hotels and most market stalls, do not accept credit card payment.

HEALTH, SAFETY & CRIME

It is not necessary to take any special health precautions while travelling in Belgium. Tap water is safe to drink, but do not drink any water from surrounding lakes or rivers as the region is not known for its commitment to environmentalism. Many Belgians prefer bottled mineral water. *Pharmacies/apotheeks* are marked by a large green cross. Belgian pharmacists are always well stocked and staff can provide expert advice.

The standard of Belgian healthcare is good, but it is not free. In most cases your travel insurance should provide the coverage you need. A European Health Insurance Card (EHIC) – which replaced the E111 form – entitles you to free or cost-reduced medical treatment in EU countries.

As in any other big cities, crime is a fact of life in Brussels. Petty theft (bag-snatching, pickpocketing) is the most common form of trouble for tourists. However, you are unlikely to experience violence or assault.

🛈 Always lock your car, and never leave valuables lying visibly.

🛈 The inner city at night is fairly safe. Your hotel can advise you about particular areas to avoid. In general, avoid the streets around Brussels Nord and Brussels Midi railway stations late at night.

❶ Carry your wallet in your front pocket, keep bags closed at all times, never leave valuables on the ground when you are seated at a table, and always wear camera bags and purses crossed over your chest.

For details of emergency numbers, refer to the 'Emergencies' section on page 136.

OPENING HOURS

Most businesses open 09.00–18.00 Monday–Friday. Department stores sometimes stay open until 21.00 on Fridays, while smaller boutiques actually close early on the same day. Generally, shops do not open on Sunday or public holidays. Banks open at 09.00 and close between 15.00 and 17.00 Monday–Friday. Cultural institutions close for one day each week – usually Mondays. Standard opening hours are 09.00–17.00. Only the biggest and most popular sights remain open seven days a week.

Usual post office opening hours are 08.00–19.00 Monday–Friday and 09.30–15.00 Saturday. The exception is the central post office on Groenplaats, which has slightly restricted hours.

TOILETS

At airports, railway stations and major tourist points, you should not have too much of a problem finding toilets. Belgians have stocked their cities with loos and most are sparkling clean. Most locals, when pressed, resort to using facilities at cafés, restaurants and bars, though it is expected that you leave a tip of between 10 and 50 cents in the white dish that you will invariably find just inside the entrance.

❶ Be warned: many of the public facilities are unisex

CHILDREN

Belgium is generally a child-friendly place. Most restaurants welcome them, and some even have play corners or outdoor playgrounds. There is often a children's menu with portions to go with the normal menu. Nappies and other handy baby articles are readily obtained from supermarkets or pharmacies (*pharmacies, apotheeks*).

If you are looking for some great places to keep the little ones occupied and amused, there's no shortage of options. **Musée des Enfants** (ⓐ Rue du Bourgmestre 15 ⓣ 02 640 0107 ⓦ www.museedesenfants.be) is an interactive children's museum in the heart of Ixelles. After a day of browsing around the markets, bring the zenith of your family's evolutionary achievement here and let them express themselves through the media of puzzles, paints, modelling clay and even an adventure playground. Try to avoid it on Sundays, when it can be absolutely packed. **Bruparck** (ⓐ Avenue du Football 1 ⓣ 02 478 0550 ⓦ www.bruparck.com) is an attraction and theme park at the base of the Atomium. Rides here include a giant Ferris wheel, plus a cinema complex and water slides. Bring patience and lots of cash. **Scientastic Museum** (ⓐ Underground level 1, Bourse, Boulevard Anspach ⓣ 02 732 1336 ⓦ www.scientastic.com) is an interactive science museum with workshops and hands-on experiments.

COMMUNICATIONS
Internet

Internet cafés are hard to come by in the centre of Brussels. Most hotels now offer broadband and/or Wi-Fi access to

guests. Sometimes this is free; sometimes a charge is made.
Flanders Tourist Information Office (⒜ Rue du Marché aux
Herbes 61–63 ☎ 02 504 0390), just off the Grand Place, has
several terminals that provide visitors with free Internet access
for 15 minutes.

Phone

Coin-operated public phones are rare; far more common are card-
operated ones. Telephone cards can be bought at any post office
and some shops (e.g. bookshops or kiosks at railway stations). A
display shows how much credit is left. Instructions on how to use
public telephones are written in English in phone booths for
international calls. Otherwise, lift up the receiver, insert the
telephone card and dial the number.

TELEPHONING BELGIUM

The code for dialling Belgium from abroad, after the access
code (00 in most countries), is 32. You then omit the initial
zero of the area code before dialling the rest of the number.
Within Belgium, you must always dial the whole number
(including area code), even when dialling a local number.

TELEPHONING ABROAD

Dial the international code you require and drop the initial
zero of the area code you're ringing. The international dialling
code for calls from Belgium to Australia is 00 61, to the UK
00 44, to the Irish Republic 00 353, to South Africa 00 27,
to New Zealand 00 64, and to the USA and Canada 001.

Post

Postal services are quick and efficient. Stamps can be bought at the numerous post offices or from automatic vending machines. Postboxes are yellow. Letters less than 50 g cost about 54 cents to Belgium, 80 cents to other EU countries, or 90 cents to all other destinations.

Central Post Office ⓐ Centre Monnaie, Place de la Monnaie
ⓣ 02 226 2111 ⓒ 08.00–19.00 Mon–Fri, 09.00–15.00 Sat
Ⓜ Metro: De Brouckère

ELECTRICITY

The standard electrical current is 220 volts. Two-pin adaptors can be purchased at most electrical shops.

TRAVELLERS WITH DISABILITIES

Facilities for visitors with disabilities are generally quite good and are usually indicated by a blue pictogram of a person in a wheelchair. In all towns and cities there are reserved car parks for wheelchair users. Motorway service stops, airports, main railway stations and most trains have suitable toilet facilities. Furthermore, many cinemas, theatres, museums and public buildings are accessible and hotels in Brussels are mostly wheelchair-friendly. However, you will need to make a request when you book. For further advice on facilities in Brussels, contact the tourist office. One word of warning for wheelchair users: many of Belgium's streets are cobblestoned.

A useful source of advice when in Brussels is **Vlaamse Federatie voor Gehandicapten** ⓐ Sint-Jansstraat 32–38
ⓣ 02 515 0262 ⓦ www.vfg.be

Useful websites

Ⓦ www.sath.org (US-based site)

Ⓦ www.access-able.com (general advice on worldwide travel)

TOURIST INFORMATION

There are two excellent tourist offices that serve Brussels: one deals with queries about the city; the other deals with queries about the province. Maps and information are eagerly distributed by the friendly and efficient English-speaking staff.

Brussels International Tourism & Congress Ⓐ Hôtel de Ville, Grand Place Ⓣ 02 513 8940 Ⓦ www.brusselsinternational.be Ⓛ 09.00–18.00 daily (summer); 09.00–18.00 Mon–Sat (winter) Ⓝ Metro: Gare Centrale

Toerisme Vlaanderen Ⓐ Rue du Marché aux Herbes 61–63 Ⓣ 02 504 0390 Ⓦ www.belgium-tourism.net Ⓛ 09.00–18.00 Mon–Sat, 09.00–17.00 Sun (summer); 09.00–17.00 Mon–Sat, 10.00–16.00 Sun (winter) Ⓝ Metro: Gare Centrale

BACKGROUND READING

Amoenitates Belgicae by Charles Baudelaire. These scathing poems attacking Belgium and its residents might put you off a visit, but their humour and passion can't be denied.

The Dutch Revolt by Geoffrey Parker. Excellent historical chronicle of the happenings that led to the end of the Spanish empire in the Low Countries during the 16th century.

The Professor by Charlotte Brontë. This first novel by Brontë is set in Brussels, and struggled to find a publisher. Not as strong as her later works, it is still an interesting chronicle of Belgian society life.

A Tall Man in a Low Land by Harry Pearson. Witty travel writing providing entertaining takes on modern Belgian life and etiquette.

Tintin by Hergé. Read any of the illustrated books from the Tintin series to discover the colourful comic traditions of the country.

Vanity Fair by William Makepeace Thackeray. While not solely devoted to Belgium, the middle of the novel features delicious descriptions of society life in Brussels immediately prior to the Battle of Waterloo.

Emergencies

The following are emergency free-call numbers:
Ambulance 100
Fire brigade 100
Police 101
General emergency number 112

MEDICAL SERVICES

Most doctors in Belgium speak at least basic English. All will be expensive, so make sure you have a European Health Insurance Card (if you are from the EU) and/or private travel insurance. Prescription and non-prescription drugs (including aspirin) are only sold at pharmacies. Most pharmacies open 09.00–18.00 Monday to Friday and 09.30–15.00 Saturday.

Hospitals

Hôpital Brugmann ⓐ Place van Gehuchten 4 ⓣ 02 477 2010 Ⓝ Metro: Houba-Brugmann
Hôpital Erasme ⓐ Route de Lennik 808 ⓣ 02 555 3111 Ⓝ Metro: Erasme
Hôpital St-Pierre ⓐ Rue Haute 322 ⓣ 02 535 3111 Ⓝ Metro: Porte de Hal

POLICE

If you lose anything or suspect that it has been stolen, then go straight to the nearest police station. While there, you will need to make a statement and fill in the required forms for insurance purposes. The central police station is located at ⓐ Rue du Marché au Charbon 30 ⓣ 02 279 7979

EMERGENCY PHRASES

Help!	**Fire!**	**Stop!**
Au secours!	Au feu!	Stop!
Ossercoor!	*Oh fur!*	*Stop!*

Call an ambulance/a doctor/the police/the fire service!
Appelez une ambulance/un médecin/la police/les pompiers!
*Ahperleh ewn ahngbewlahngss/ang medesang/lah poleess/
leh pompeeyeh!*

EMBASSIES & CONSULATES

Australian Embassy ⓐ Rue Guimard 6–8 ⓣ 02 286 0500
ⓦ www.austemb.be ⓛ 08.30–17.00 Mon–Fri

British Embassy ⓐ Rue d'Arlon 85 ⓣ 02 287 6211
ⓦ www.britishembassy.gov.uk/belgium ⓛ 09.00–17.30 Mon–Fri

Irish Embassy ⓐ Rue Wiertz 50, Brussels ⓣ 02 235 6676
ⓦ www.irlgov.ie/iveagh ⓛ 10.00–13.00 Mon–Fri

New Zealand Embassy ⓐ Seventh floor, Square de Meeûs 1
ⓣ 02 512 1040 ⓦ www.nzembassy.com/belgium
ⓛ 09.00–13.00, 14.00–17.30 Mon–Fri

Republic of South Africa Embassy ⓐ Rue Montoyer 17
ⓣ 02 285 4400 ⓦ www.southafrica.be ⓛ 08.30–17.00 Mon–Fri

US Embassy ⓐ Boulevard du Régent 27, Etterbeek ⓣ 02 508 2111
ⓦ www.usembassy.be ⓛ 09.00–18.00 Mon–Fri

INDEX

ACKNOWLEDGEMENTS

The publishers would like to thank the following for providing their copyright photographs for this book: Anwer Bati pages 5, 40–41, 64, 103, 125; dreamstime page 79; iStock photos page 75; jmerelo page 30; Visit Flanders pages 33, 47; Neil Setchfield all others.

Project editor: Diane Teillol
Layout: Julie Crane
Proofreaders: Caroline Hunt & Jan McCann

The updater would like to thank Sophie Bouallègue and Amanda Monroe for their help in updating this book.

Send your thoughts to
books@thomascook.com

- **Found a great bar, club, shop or must-see sight that we don't feature?**
- **Like to tip us off about any information that needs a little updating?**
- **Want to tell us what you love about this handy little guidebook and more importantly how we can make it even handier?**

Then here's your chance to tell all! Send us ideas, discoveries and recommendations today and then look out for your valuable input in the next edition of this title.

Email the above address (stating the title) or write to:
pocket guides Series Editor, Thomas Cook Publishing, PO Box 227, Coningsby Road, Peterborough PE3 8SB, UK.

WHAT'S IN YOUR GUIDEBOOK?

Independent authors Impartial up-to-date information from our travel experts who meticulously source local knowledge.

Experience Thomas Cook's 165 years in the travel industry and guidebook publishing enriches every word with expertise you can trust.

Travel know-how Thomas Cook has thousands of staff working around the globe, all living and breathing travel.

Editors Travel-publishing professionals, pulling everything together to craft a perfect blend of words, pictures, maps and design.

You, the traveller We deliver a practical, no-nonsense approach to information, geared to how you really use it.

Useful phrases

English	French	Approx pronunciation
BASICS		
Yes	Oui	*Wee*
No	Non	*Nawng*
Please	S'il vous plaît	*Sylvooplay*
Thank you	Merci	*Mehrsee*
Hello	Bonjour	*Bawngzhoor*
Goodbye	Au revoir	*Aw revwahr*
Excuse me	Excusez-moi	*Ekskewzeh-mwah*
Sorry	Désolé(e)	*Dehzoleh*
That's okay	Ça va	*Sahr vahr*
I don't speak French	Je ne parle pas français	*Zher ner pahrl pah frahngsay*
Do you speak English?	Parlez-vous anglais?	*Pahrlay-voo ohnglay?*
Good morning	Bonjour	*Bawng-zhoor*
Good afternoon	Bonjour	*Bawng-zhoor*
Good evening	Bonsoir	*Bawng-swah*
Goodnight	Bonne nuit	*Bun nwee*
My name is ...	Je m'appelle ...	*Zher mahpehl ...*
NUMBERS		
One	Un/Une	*Uhn/Oon*
Two	Deux	*Dur*
Three	Trois	*Trwah*
Four	Quatre	*Kahtr*
Five	Cinq	*Suhnk*
Six	Six	*Seess*
Seven	Sept	*Seht*
Eight	Huit	*Weet*
Nine	Neuf	*Nurf*
Ten	Dix	*Deess*
Twenty	Vingt	*Vuhng*
Fifty	Cinquante	*Suhngkahnt*
One hundred	Cent	*San*
SIGNS & NOTICES		
Airport	Aéroport	*Ahehrohpohr*
Rail station	Gare	*Gahr*
Platform	Quai	*Kay*
Smoking/	Permit de fumer/	*Permee der foom-eh/*
No smoking	Interdit de fumer	*Anterdee der foom-eh*
Toilets	Toilettes	*Twahlaitt*
Ladies/Gentlemen	Femmes/Hommes	*Fam/Ommh*
Subway/Bus	Métro/Bus	*Maytroa/Booss*